THE
WRITER'S
INTERNET
HANDBOOK

TIMOTHY K. MALOY

ALLWORTH PRESS
NEW YORK

Published by Allworth Press
An imprint of Allworth Communications
10 East 23rd Street, New York, NY 10010

Cover design by Douglas Designs, New York, NY

Book Design by Sharp Des!gns, Holt, MI

ISBN: 1-880559-80-3

Library of Congress Catalog Card Number: 96-84656

Table of Contents

Introduction: New Territory

Tell me, O muse, of that ingenious hero who traveled far and wide after he had sacked the famous town of Troy. Many cities did he visit, and many were the nations with whose manners and customs he was acquainted; moreover, he suffered much by sea while trying to save his own life and bring his men safely home; but do what he might he could not save his men, for they perished through their own sheer folly in eating the cattle of the Sun-god Hyperion; so the god prevented them from ever reaching home. Tell me, too, about all these things, O daughter of Jove, from whatsoever source you may know them.

—*The Odyssey,* by Homer (800 B.C.), translated by Samuel Butler.

Found at: *http://darkwing.uoregon.edu/~joelja/odyssey.html*

Thus begins what is considered to be one of the first great narrative works ever crafted—the sublime story of a man just trying to get home. Homer begins this story—as many writers do—by evoking the muse, a force of creativity and divine inspiration. As I embarked upon *The Writer's Internet Handbook,* I was curious about how I should begin, and I thought that an invocation of the muse would prove most effective. As muses are hardly handy in these modern times, I thought who better to lean on for inspiration than my friend Homer.

But could he and his muse be called upon via the Internet? With little trouble—just a few unmatriculated online wanderings through university classics departments—I did indeed find *The Odyssey, The Iliad,* their muse, and their author Homer. It was an ineffable moment when those fiery words from several thousand years ago appeared upon my terminal as if by Olympian design. How wonderful that, in addition to being told in the agora and later sold in bookstores, these stories are now available for reading on the Net.

Which brings us to the point of this introduction: writers should look upon the Internet not as a technology to be mastered, but as *tool* that can help them creatively and commercially. Homer and all the other authors, famous or obscure, whose writings have been digitally archived at Websites and on the Internet, contribute to the content that makes up the Net. And in the end, it is its *content* that gives the Internet its value.

Tailor-Made for Writers

Depending on how you look at this globe-darting giant, the Internet is a medium tailor-made for writers. The Internet and its most renowned cousin, the World Wide Web, is almost as capacious as infinity itself, and in this infinitude there is a voracious need for content. The rise of the Net was anticipated by a number of writers, most notably science fiction writer William Gibson, who coined the term *cyberspace,* which has become the all-purpose moniker used to describe the otherwise hard-to-name guts of the Internet. While the Net was invented by scientists, its "invention" in the popular imagination was midwifed by writers such as Gibson who anticipated that one day such a medium for communication would come into being.

Through e-mail, for example, you can exchange ideas, trade resources, and carry on correspondence with fellow writers; authors can participate in group discussions through Usenet Newsgroups and Listservs, both of which are now famous for the proliferation of affinity groups through the Net.

Writers can use the Net's e-mail function to contact editors and submit drafts or finished pieces to clients and potential clients—instantaneously. These conveniences alone are reason enough to get Net access. On the Net, writers will also find many newly launched publications that can prove more accessible to aspiring writers in search of amenable publishers. As we set out, remember that the Internet is a writerly place. And even more importantly, it's filled with potential readers.

In *The Writer's Internet Handbook,* I will show that there is a growing world of publishing that has completely departed from hard copy (offline) and is venturing boldly into the online world. I will also show how to access this new online frontier—whether it be the online edition of a newspaper, a Web magazine, an alternative e-zine, e-mail "newsletters," online content packaged along with an information service, or text for interactive Websites. Best of all, you can bypass the middleman entirely and publish material yourself, thus going straight to your readers online.

All this *new media* means more possible venues for writers and more freedom, but it also requires a few new skills. It is helpful to be familiar with the various facets of the Net and the basics of Internet publishing in order to reach your audience. The body of *The Writer's Internet Handbook* aims to help writers find and make use of the opportunities and resources available on the Internet. For those new to the Net, a guide to the basics of getting connected and finding your way around the Internet is provided in the Appendix. The Appendix also contains a glossary of Internet terms and lists of resources and helpful contact addresses.

The primary vehicle for publishing via the Net is the World Wide Web, which is comprised of Websites with "pages" that can contain all text or a mixture of text with pictures, sound, and video. In chapter 16, Web page designer Thomas Timmons provides a relatively quick and easy guide to creating a Website. He explains the basics of hypertext markup language (HTML), the language used to lay out a Web page. While new authoring software has made it possible to create a Website without a thorough knowledge of HTML, familiarity with the basics will greatly increase your ability to create a Website that fits your needs. It also will make you a more competitive writer in the online market.

Whether you're a lone-wolf writer or with an organization, the world of new media often requires a capacity to perform tasks that formerly were done by separate individuals. Writers used to mail their manuscripts to magazines or publishers that would take care of the meat and potatoes of turning the manuscript into a book—editing, copyediting, design, and production. Today, online, these tasks often fall to the writer. The Internet, therefore, offers writers both new freedom and new challenges. If writers rise to the challenge, they will discover that they have gained more responsibility, but also more *control* over the finished product.

In the chapters that follow, we will wander Odysseus-like through the many features of the Internet. It might help to think of each chapter as a distinct island emerging from the sea of information on the Net, providing a view from which writers can gain information and experience. The Internet is young and mostly uncharted. The writers who will benefit most from this book will be wily and resourceful like our Homeric hero, men and women of "many ways" who creatively apply themselves to using the Internet as a tool in their writing careers.

■

Writers and the New Media

My linen suit was already wrinkling on that humid day of the summer solstice as I entered the Explorers Hall of the National Geographic Society in Washington, D.C. Once in the door, I was directed toward an array of computers where Netsurfers sat mesmerized by the glowing screens, occasionally sipping from their coffees. I was offered a genuine pith helmet and led to my own computer in the Society's new cybercafé, where I began to Netsurf. I began with a quick online jaunt through South Africa, including some digressions into detailed material about specific animals; then a more extended trip to the Caribbean to hunt for treasures on a sunken Spanish galleon; my final click carried me to the cartographic center, where I perused the maps for which the National Geographic Society is so well known.

As a professional journalist, I felt as if I were on assignment with the famed *National Geographic* writers, photographers, and mapmakers whom I had grown up worshipping. I had seen many Web sites over the last few years—some of glamorous design and others with endless content—but here was one of the few that combined style and substance. Welcome to *National Geographic* online, I thought. With the launch of its Web locale (*http://www.nationalgeographic.com*), the esteemed National Geographic Society turned a new page in its 108-year history that once again will keep it at the forefront of people's minds.

"It's very interactive, unlike anything that's ever been seen," said Reg Murphy, president of the Society. "People come away with a taste of what it's like to be out in the field with explorers, sort of like having a digital pith helmet."

An example of Murphy's claim can be seen in one of the premier adventures offered online, where National Geographic takes Net users along for an actual expedition to recover gold, silver, and other artifacts from the galleon *Concepción* sunken off the coast of the Dominican Republic.

During the ongoing expedition, the underwater explorers send along written and photographic updates of their recovery efforts, which are added to the Web exhibits about their adventure. It is this kind of continual filing of news that makes the Geographic's new Net site different, in part, from the famous yellow-bordered magazine that is enjoyed by millions of readers and then stored in attics or basements with almost religious fervor.

Interactive and updated, the plans for the Geographic Web site is to offer content closely allied with the features appearing in the *National Geographic* and *Traveler* magazines, along with material from the *Explorer* television series.

This is but one example of the new media that is calling out to writers now and into the twenty-first century.

New Media

New media has become one of the most bandied about terms in recent years. And like many of the new words and phrases that pertain to computers and high tech in general, it can mean several things at once. For the purposes of this book, the term *new media* means just that. There are old media such as books, newspapers, television, and cable, and, now, there is a new kind of media in the form of digital information. New media is new, in part, because it often combines many of the elements of the old media and synergizes them into a greater whole.

This book attempts to get a handle on where the ancient art of writing fits into this world of new media on the Internet. What we are really looking at is the importance of the Internet to writers—from journalists and freelancers to ghostwriters, public relations communicators, essayists, poets, and novelists. To start, let's look at some examples of the new media spawned by the Internet and, at the same time, how the old media is adapting to this new frontier.

This partial list of Internet addresses hints at the variety of resources for writers available on the Net.

- The American Library Association: *http://www.ala.org*
- Bookwire: *http://www.bookwire.com*
- Amazon.com Bookstore: *http://www.amazon.com*
- *Wired* magazine: *http://www.hotwired.com*
- Word: *http://www.word.com*
- Zuzu's Petals Literary Resources: *http://www.lehigh.net/zuzu*

A whole world of information has been made available by the almost unimaginably quick expansion of Internet use around the world. This is important to writers because the Internet represents an unprecedented market for readable content that must be generated by all types of writers. While the Net is filled with multimedia content in the form of sound, pictures, and video, the real backbone of Net content is writing.

This is most obvious in the case of the old media, which republishes a great deal of its content on the World Wide Web portion of the Internet. A writer for the *Boston Globe* (*http://www.boston.com*), who previously found herself well known among readers in New England, might, through the Internet, suddenly find her stories being read in Ireland. Conversely, Ireland's leading newspaper, the *Irish Times* (*http://www.irish-times.ie*), has been published on the Web since 1995, and, therefore, its writers can be, and are, read throughout the world. Via the *Irish Times* online, readers around the globe can check on anything from soccer scores and weather to business news relevant to the Republic of Ireland.

There are many online newspapers besides the *Boston Globe* and *Irish Times*. A more recent addition to the world of online editions is *SunSpot* (*http://www.sunspot.net*), the Web version of the venerable *Baltimore Sun* and a great deal more.

"*SunSpot* is Maryland's online community. It's a lively and usable Web site that provides practical links to nearly any kind of information," says *SunSpot* publisher Lawrence Kessler. "It's also a great place

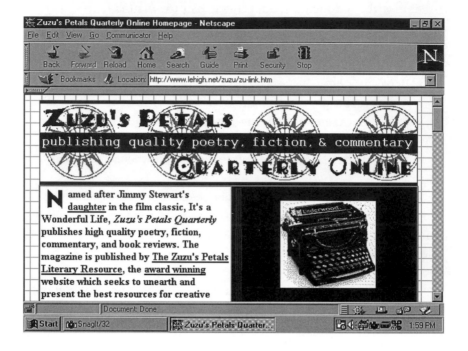

At Zuzu's Petals, a complete literary resource, it's a wonderful life for writers.

to hang out, exchange thoughts, contribute ideas, and explore the wonderful offerings of the Web while connecting with various communities of interest in our region."

While Kessler's comments reflect his obvious pride in *SunSpot*, his comments also reflect the fact that he is the publisher of something entirely different from the hard copy edition of the *Baltimore Sun*. How is it different? In brief, the *SunSpot* Web site broadens the already large scope of information being published by its parent newspaper. For instance, like many Internet newspapers, *SunSpot* provides a vast regional electronic marketplace in the form of searchable classifieds. If you are looking, let's say, for a 1962 Ford Galaxy Sunline, you can enter those words while netsurfing *SunSpot*'s classifieds, and they will match up with just such a car—if one happens to be for sale. This is far easier than scanning printed classifieds, and the information is updated continually, not gathered and published each day or week. As in any typical classified section—in addition to cars—boats, stereos, musical instruments, antiques, pets, and countless other items are offered for sale. All are searchable by location, color, price, make, model, or "almost any specification that fits the user's requirements," Kessler says. There are also job and real estate listings.

SunSpot features real-time sports updates, which, like watching television or listening to the radio, keep you updated on the latest scores. Unlike TV or radio, however, you have access to scores of games on demand, including some that might not be available in your viewing or listening area.

There are a variety of online discussion forums in *SunSpot*, including a comprehensive statewide events calendar and a searchable arts and entertainment calendar; there is even a local soap opera called "Beehive" that is set in Baltimore. The events section is called "Our Town," and the most interactive section of *SunSpot*—where the forums and "Beehive" are situated—is called the "Crabhouse." *SunSpot* promises that at the "Crabhouse" one can "Engage in a poetry slam, explore the art scene, talk with local celebrities, or enter a contest of skills."

Perhaps most importantly, there is the news of the day—local, national, and international—with constant updates. You can get late-breaking news, international weather, stock quotes, and more.

Mary Junck, publisher of the *Baltimore Sun*, says that this new cyberprogeny will help the newspaper stay competitive as an information provider for people living in the Mid-Atlantic region. "With *SunSpot*, we are finding new ways to serve our customers, both readers and advertisers. *SunSpot* provides information and news, but it also brings services, resources, and the entire community into people's homes, offices, and schools," Junck said. "*SunSpot* grows the *Sun*'s franchise beyond the newspaper's traditional audience."

If you would like to browse through the thousands of national and international newspapers on the Net, the journalism magazine *Editor and Publisher*'s excellent Web site (*http://wwww.mediainfo.com*) will help you to do so.

Television, Cable, and New Media

When it comes to conventional media adapting to the new media, newspapers aren't the whole story. What about television? Indeed, a quick jaunt through news media on the Web reveals that each of the large networks—ABC, NBC, CBS, and Fox—have excellent newsy Web sites. Big cable outfits like CNN also have become major forces on the Net. And several hundred local TV stations have Web sites of their own that can be accessed via a link site (*http://www.newslink.org*).

This "repurposing of content" has turned broadcasters into *publishers.* Now, instead of hearing anchors read the news, we can read not only the text used in broadcast, but longer, in-depth stories as well— a new market for writers made possible by the low cost of publishing on the Net and the interactive features that allow readers a greater range of choice.

March Gunther, in an article about online journalism for the *American Journalism Review*, writes: "On a typical weekday afternoon, Allison Davis, a former producer for NBC's *Today,* is leading a tiny band of cyberjournalists who are bringing NBC news into the online world. In cramped quarters strewn with computer cables and phone lines, they are preparing stories on Bosnia and Medicare. NBC correspondents write an analysis of Time Warner's merger with Turner Broadcasting and select audio clips and still pictures from a Katie Couric interview with House Speaker Newt Gingrich," he writes. "Within hours, the stories, pictures, and clips will be uploaded into a vast storehouse of information . . . on the Net."

Special events contribute further to the growth of new media. For example, numerous media giants fielded Web sites solely to keep Netsurfers and political junkies fully informed about the 1996 presidential race, the battle for control of Congress, and hundreds of local contests. Among the powerhouse sites were: Politics Now, a joint venture of ABC News, the *National Journal*, *Newsweek*, and the *Washington Post*; AllPolitics, which was jointly operated by CNN and *Time* magazine; and the MSNBC Web site put together by Microsoft and NBC News.

Each of those political Web sites employed skilled teams of writers, reporters, and editors who covered the campaign and then put their stories on the Internet. They were good sites, especially useful for residents of areas where there was no easy access to major metropolitan newspapers. These political sites picked up a large following of Netsurfers as the campaign continued; so many, in fact, that the sites got overloaded on election night when millions of people tried to access them for results.

Olympic Coverage

A similar explosion of new media came about with the creation of various Web sites that covered the 1996 Olympics. The Olympic Games in Atlanta were epic in many ways, notably by the number of countries participating, the unprecedented amount of viewers worldwide, the volume of tickets sold, and the vast array of Internet pages that covered the event.

The Olympics, like many world-class events in the years since the Internet has come of age, provided yet another chance for the new media to employ the Net for ground-breaking coverage of the proceedings. Here's a close look at how the new media handled the Olympics. This was the first Olympics to be put on the Web and the technology passed the test for garnering a large audience share and for disseminating information.

There were some big players in the field of Internet Olympic coverage. NBC was the obvious leader of the pack. As the network had the television rights to the event, it found itself in the natural position to provide some of the top Net coverage. However, CNN was also on the Net with the Olympics as the centerpiece of its Web pages;

ESPN put out an excellent set of Net pages during the event; and the new NBC companion network MSNBC published well-regarded Olympic Net pages.

Other big fish included IBM, the official technology provider for the games, and phone giant AT&T, which also fielded a comprehensive set of Net pages covering the events. And if that wasn't enough, many of the major daily newspapers—*USA Today*, the *New York Times*, and the home-grown *Atlanta Constitution*—were substantial Olympic information providers through the Net. The list goes on, including special sites devoted exclusively to women's sports (*http://womensports. com*) and others that followed specific events, such as one that focused on soccer. All this is to say that for the first Net Olympiad, there was no lack of information for those who wanted to follow the event from their desktop computers.

Various Web and media analysts rated NBC, CNN, ESPNet, IBM, and AT&T as the top Olympic Web sites. Interesting, of course, is the fact that IBM, a technology company, and AT&T, a telecommunications provider, both emerged as information broadcasters. But that is the nature of the new media world created by the Net.

USA Today reporter Leslie Miller wrote the following of NBC's site after a poll of veteran Netsurfers: "About three hundred regular Web surfers rated NBC tops in visual appeal, ease of use, and up-to-date content, among other categories."

Beth Howard, NBC Interactive's Olympic producer, said that planning for the Network's Olympiad Web pages began the summer before the contests, and that the site was then launched in January as a long-term preview to the event.

While praising the result of all this advance planning, Howard described putting the event online as "a learning experience." She added, however, that the final structure and content of NBC's Olympic pages "confirmed our beliefs" that the network did its best job when concentrating on the many stories that were part of the games. "Whenever we wrote an article [for the Web pages], it was about storytelling," she said. "Our mission was to bring the magic of the Olympics back to our audience." Howard reported that the most visited section of NBC's Olympic page was the "Athlete of the Week" and "Athlete of the Day" pages. Overall, the Web pages received five to several million "hits" per day.

For Jeff Gerrard, executive producer at CNN Interactive, the Internet coverage of such a large-scale event came off well, but he also suggested to all others contemplating comprehensive Web coverage, "Like any big project, you can't start too early with your planning. We spent three months developing each of our different [Olympic] sections," he said. "We tried to build a lot of pages to cover all the sports."

And there is still a large learning curve for Web coverage, Gerrard said. "Television is a mature technology, it's either live or on tape and you sent it out. On the Web, you are becoming like a software company in that it involves programming—you have to think in terms of beta testing, development cycles, just like a software company."

He praised the new paradigm of Internet coverage as eliminating the time restrictions encountered in TV and cable broadcasting because a producer can keep creating new pages for each sport as it is up to the user which page they want to see and how much time they spend. "We can really cover everything," said Gerrard, comparing Net pages to sports that got short-shrifted in television coverage. "I think it's a great way to present news, including sports." According to CNN spokeswoman Dawn Echols, CNN recorded 111 million hits on its Internet site by the time of the tragic bombing that took place at the Olympics.

From Tabula Rasa to Full Slate

New media crossovers from conventional publishing and broadcasting make up but a small portion of the Internet's content. Web sites have emerged covering almost any conceivable subject. Many of these sites are maintained by a single person or small-interest group, but the new media has also spawned its own Internet-based publishing ventures. Probably of most interest to writers are the crop of new Web magazines that have sprung up on the Net.

"Part of our mission is to bring cyberspace down to earth," declares Michael Kinsley in the opening address of his new online offering, *Slate*, backed by the Microsoft Corporation. *Slate* is a Web magazine that puts emphasis on the text versus the "hyper." As in a standard print magazine, long and substantial written pieces are the mainstay of the features appearing in this publication, and the staff of writers include a constellation of scribes from the journalistic establishment.

Unlike the numerous publications that start as hard copy and then reprint the same text in digital form, *Slate* began as an online magazine. A text-file version of *Slate* can be downloaded and printed from the Web pages, and there are plans to sell a conventional hard-copy version of *Slate* through the Starbucks coffee empire. The "paper" edition of *Slate* will sell for $29 yearly. This heralds a new paradigm in the publishing world whereby a publication makes its debut on the World Wide Web and then also produces on offline adjunct to the online original.

Slate has the jump on many Web magazines in the solid journalistic imprint of Michael Kinsley, who doesn't hail originally from the digital world. But who does hail completely from the digital world, which in many senses is all of three or four years old? *Slate* has been accused of being staid in comparison to many other online offerings, which tend to have more youthful and self-consciously hip writing, design, and technological staff. The magazine will probably evolve with time. Perhaps it will take on more of the trappings of the digital world, but, for the time being, Web publications like *Slate* have had the effect of redirecting attention toward the uncomplicated presentation of content. Quick comparisons to some very credible online offerings would include *Salon*, *Feed*, and *Urban Desires* (see URL locations below.)

Unlike the majority of Web magazines, *Slate* plans eventually to charge for its content, $19.95 a year for the cyberversion. "We believe that expecting readers to share the cost, as they do in print, is the only way serious journalism on the Web can be self-supporting," Kinsley says in his opening salutation. "Depending completely on advertisers would not be healthy even it were possible." But, one will find from viewing *Slate* that it seems to suffer no lack of advertiser interest.

To see *Slate* and other literary Web magazines, go to these URLs:
- *Slate:* http://www.slate.com
- *Salon:* http://www.salon1999.com
- *Feed:* http://www.feedmag.com
- *Urban Desires:* http://www.desires.com

Wrap Up

This is just a small glimpse into the world of new media, and it is a world of writers. Magazines, newsletters, newspapers, and, quite importantly, television news organizations, are being staffed with new media writers who understand the changing concept of writing as it applies to going online with text and multimedia.

News writers and just plain writers who understand the world of global, electronic information spread—who understand that there is an information explosion afoot—will find themselves more employable in the coming years. Why? Because the writing market is larger than ever, with more prospects for selling, and there is a demand for writing on more topics for global, regional, and local audiences.

Let's start by looking at just the local. You are a writer, let's say, who follows the local scene, including anything from music, theater, and movies to festivals and other local events. In the near future, more often than not, citizens of any particular locale will jump onto the Internet to get this type of local information. Whether from a desktop computer, Internet-connected television, or, even more likely, a small, personal "information device," people will get their information via electronic means.

The demand to know what's going on locally—be it schedules or reviews—will be (and is being) satisfied by writers who are writing for the new media. And these writers can come from all the nooks and crannies of the writing world. They need not be with a newspaper or online news organization. They could be writing for a community theater organization offering a backstage look at what went into producing a current play. They could be with a local sports team, writing player profiles for public consumption; a school board member who has a regular online column about school issues; creative writers spinning plots for online soap operas like *SunSpot*'s "Beehive"; or writers working in any of a number of genres.

There is a demand for all this content, and it is salable as a product on the Internet. Later we look at how the Net can help journalists and other writers disseminate their material and get paid for it.

Catherine Fulton, writing in the *Columbia Journalism Review,* said the following about new media and how it changes—and possibly broadens—the field for writers. "Changing technologies force journalists to reexamine what they do and why. What exactly is news, and who has the right to report it? How do you make it useful? Do people select and absorb information differently in the online environment? Every new media service has to ask questions like these. The answers will create a new generation of journalistic conventions that could well affect old media as well. New technologies, therefore, give journalistic reformers an ideal opening to try new ideas."

■

Publishing and Profiting in the New Media

Most of the new media ventures mentioned in the first chapter were able to launch themselves and continue running during their less profitable start-up phases because they had old-media parents with deep pockets. These parents do, however, expect their new-media children to make money in the near future. And, in many cases, these ventures are well beyond their first tentative baby steps in generating revenue, paying for themselves, and even cutting a profit.

But there have also been some losses. One of the biggest and earliest ventures in publishing material online was undertaken by media giant Time Warner with its well-known Pathfinder site on the World Wide Web. While this vast Web locale—comprised of literally hundreds of thousands of pages—gained quick recognition and many readers, it is (as of this writing) still operating well in the red. It was reported in 1996 that this venture spent $15 million on Web publishing while taking in only $3 million. This is not an example to follow.

This cautionary example aside, there are many Web publishing ventures, big and small, that are either showing the potential for lucrative profits or are already well within the black on their balance sheets. This prognosis of financial well-being among potential new media clients is good news for writers, but writers should also think of online publishing as an opportunity to take a more active role in promoting their own work. Unlike larger publishing groups, individual writers usually have little to lose in creating their own Web presence. We will take a look at some of the ways that writers can use Web publishing to make money from their material. In particular, we will look at how those with a literary bent can start their own "publishing houses" on the Net, and profit by doing so.

The Individual Writer

Robert Seidman is a good example of a creative scribe who used the new media to make a successful career for himself as a professional writer. Seidman did not start out as a writer. He held positions at Sprint, MCI, and IBM that did not require writing, but he had an interest in what was going on in cyberspace and an urge to write about it. Even better, he had an urge to cyberpublish his own column, "In, Around, and On-line." Once made available online, his writing was sufficiently readable and insightful to begin gathering readers among the Internet cognoscenti. Soon, based on the reputation he developed through his self-published online column, Seidman was offered, and accepted, a position writing for the hard-copy publication *NetGuide*— a magazine that follows the goings on inside the Internet.

Here we have an instance of someone with no formal training, coming from outside the usual channels, becoming recognized and finding a good writing job via the Net. The Internet is a tool that offers writers new avenues for building careers. At the same time, certain basic facts about writing remain the same. There is more to getting noticed, paid, or hired than just posting your personal screed on the Net. If, for instance, you want to be an online columnist, you must—like Seidman—have something interesting to say, and you must say interesting things somewhat regularly. This is the first and most essential step. On the Net, good writing is still what matters. Even if you don't get paid, you may find sympathetic readers and some level of fame by placing your material online. The point of the Seidman case is that previous barriers to publishing, such as having to find a willing publication or editor to give your career a start, have been removed by the Internet. That still leaves the *vox populi*, or "public judgment" of your work. And, in many ways, that has greater, or at least more immediate, weight on the Net than in conventional publishing. Seidman, quoted in a *Los Angeles Times* article, reminds us that in reading cyberpublished works, "You will judge this in the same way as any other medium. If you like the subject or the writing, you will keep reading, or even subscribe. Otherwise, you'll just throw it away." Robert Seidman's serendipitous plunge into a writing career is an inspiring instance of a self-published author who gained recognition through the Net.

Mind's Eye Fiction

The costs of printing and distribution have always severely limited the ability of small or upstart publishing ventures to find the market for their materials. But small publishers have recently become unchained by the rather low cost of Net publishing. Ken Jenks, creator of Mind's Eye Fiction (*http://www.tale.com/*), is one such publisher.

Mind's Eye is a Web site that allows readers to peruse the beginning portions of the articles and short stories, but then requires payment if the reader is interested in continuing. Some in the Internet press have called Mind's Eye a "tease," but Jenks has found a legitimate way to sell writing via the Net. In an interview with the *Houston Chronicle,* he explained that the whole effort was still in its infancy. "We have about a twenty-to-one ratio of lookers to buyers," Jenks said. "I'm not planning on making a profit for the first two years."

Part of the problem when it comes to the question of profitability is the fact that a paradigm for monetary transactions through the Net is still yet to be established. Profit or not, Jenks is charging for his material and Mind's Eye is receiving money. The stories are priced between 50¢ and $1, and to purchase a complete story, the "buyer" must have an account with a recently established bank for Net transactions, aptly named First Virtual Holdings.

With First Virtual, account holders are given identification numbers, which they can present at participating Web sites. When the numbers are used, First Virtual debits the account for the amount of the purchase. There are no credit card numbers involved, thus reducing the worry about losing your shirt via an online purchase (a worry that the author of this book thinks is vastly overrated).

The trouble is this: not many Netsurfers are First Virtual account holders, which limits the amount of people to whom Jenks or other

Peddling prose online, Mind's Eye Fiction is perhaps a harbinger of the future for literary Web sites.

online writers and publishers can sell. But this is changing quickly as online commerce becomes the norm rather than the exception.

Another similar venture is BiblioBytes (*http://www.bb.com*), based in Hoboken, New Jersey, and run by Glen Hauman. The Web site sells entire novels online, charging in the $3 to $5 range. Hauman says that his venture has recently become profitable.

Online Transactions

Various writer-advocacy groups, such as the National Writers Union (NWU), have taken formal positions that online transactions represent the wave of the future for selling written works and will have profound implications for individual writers. "Digital cash and other forms of online transactions make possible a new wave of financially viable self-publishing," said NWU president Jonathan Tasini. "This will help to prevent corporate publishers from completely dominating what is distributed in the commercial portions of the Internet. The ability of individual writers and informal publishing operations to sell their material to the Net will encourage greater diversity in what is distributed online."

The NWU has published a very informative paper entitled "Freelance Writers and Online Commerce," which can be found at: *http://www.nlightning.com/e-money.html*.

These technology companies and financial institutions can assist an online publisher or writer with setting up online transactions:
- Clickshare Corp: *http://www.clickshare.com*
- CyberCash: *http://www.cybercash.com*
- DigiCash: *http://www.digicash.com*
- First Virtual: *http://www.fv.com*
- Mark Twain Bank: *http://www. marktwain.com*

Advertising Income

While many different payment schemes for online information from the Net are still being worked out, there are a number of other ways that online writing and writers are finding financial support. For the last several years, a great deal of online content has gained revenue the same way it does in the offline world—through advertising.

Newspapers and television have always made money through advertising—whether "space ads" and classifieds in newspapers and magazines or commercials on television. And money is being made through advertising with new media as well.

One of the prime examples of this is the Yahoo Web site, which acts as a directory service for the Internet by categorizing the Net under topical headings. It was started by two engineering graduate students who quit school and are now running a multimillion dollar enterprise. Yahoo's primary revenue stream comes from advertising at various locales on the Web that host advertising "banners," and it charges some of the highest rates to advertisers. It can do this because the traffic at the Yahoo site is so enormous and because of the intangible, which we call "credibility," that comes from Yahoo's good reputation for being a useful service on the Internet.

Closer to home for most writers are Web publications such as *Salon* or *Feed*, which also gain revenue from advertising. Most of these advertisements appear in the form of banners, which are comparable to space ads in newspapers and magazines, but also—using the information superhighway metaphor—could be compared to roadside billboards.

There is, however, an important difference between Web banners and conventional ads. One click on these cyberadvertisements instantly leads to more information on the product or service in question. A banner for Ford Motors, for example, will tell you about this company's most recent line of vehicles. Often, banners, when clicked, provide the means for online ordering. Banners are also capable of some degree of movement, making them vaguely similar to television ads; they will change images and content before your eyes without being clicked. And, already, so-called streaming technology allows for limited use of video advertising on the Web, which makes it highly likely that more TV-like ads will begin appearing on the Web in the near future.

Various Internet industry experts and advertising analysts are all still debating which paradigm of Web advertising will prove most effective—static banners versus dynamic banners versus TV-like ads—and no doubt the forms mentioned here, and new forms, will each find their niche in time.

Hunter Madsen, vice president of commercial strategies at *Hot*

Wired (the Net version of *Wired* magazine), told a *Web Week* reporter that banner ads will continue as the chief preference of many advertisers because "they provide a uniform format for media planning and buying across a wide range of sites. They are convenient and they provide the kind of standards that media buyers are used to. There will be many variations in how they pop up, where they appear, and when they appear. But banners are going to be around for a long time."

Many rank-and-file Netsurfers are debating whether there should be ads on the Internet at all, but this is, in many ways, a moot debate. No one owns the Net, and each site can host or not host advertising as it wishes. The real effect of any *vox populi* regarding ads will be if Netsurfers visit certain Web sites or not, depending on how obtrusive the advertising is.

Nevertheless, writers contemplating the launch of any kind of Web publication, whether a zine or other Net missive, may want to explore the possibility of advertising income as at least one source of recompense for the hard work of cyberpublishing. An estimated $500 billion is expected to be spent by online advertisers by the year 2000, according to the *Wall Street Journal*.

The following is a brief list of Web publications that play host to various types of "Netvertising":

- *Feed: http://www.feedmag.com*
- *Salon: http://www.Salon1999.com*
- *Slate: http://slate.com*
- *Word: http://www.word.com*

Sponsorship

A number of Web sites that perform a variety of informative purposes and employ one or more writers have been launched with the aid of corporate sponsors who, whether for public relations reasons or because these sites are allied somehow with the sponsor, chose to support these endeavors.

One example is the *Electric Minds* Web site, which was launched in the last half of 1996 and serves a "community building" purpose in that it provides a context and forum for Netsurfers to come together and discuss technology and its impact on society. Founded by veteran

Internet guru and pundit Howard Rheingold, author of *Virtual Community* (1994), the *Electric Minds* site has secured big-name sponsors like Apple Computer and Sun Microsystems.

Above and beyond gaining operating moneys from his sponsors, Rheingold has said that he plans to also generate revenue by "repackaging" some of the discussions and articles that appear in *Electric Minds* and reselling them in a number of mediums, including good old-fashioned book form, a video series, and possibly as the basis for a cable-TV series.

It's doubtful that anyone is currently making a fortune publishing on the Web, but some small publishing ventures are indeed making money (or at least covering operating expenses) through sales, via advertising or sponsorship, and by republishing content in conventional media. The next chapter further explores the ways in which writers will benefit by maintaining an online presence.

■

3

A Place Online

This chapter deals with the value of writers maintaining Web pages for the purposes of publishing, promotion, and publicity. As a writer seeking opportunities in both the new and old media, a home page on the World Wide Web is a versatile tool that makes your writing accessible via electronic means. Creating a Web site is not brain surgery. You can buy software that will do the basic job for you, and in chapter 16 you will learn the essentials of hypertext markup language (HTML), which will allow you to create a Web site tailored to your specific needs. Creating a home page is also not costly. Most Internet service providers will give you free space for your home page, and the commercial online services, like America Online, CompuServe, and Prodigy, also provide space and help for subscriber home pages.

A home page is your way of maintaining a virtual presence. The value of having a place on the Web is not simply in self-publishing your work, but also in being able to leverage your position as a writer and gain recognition by having a presence on the Net.

Your home page can be anything from a simple means of making your résumé and some top clips available to your own self-published online magazine. One cautionary point about presenting your home page as an "electronic publication": most publications (online or offline) usually have a number of bylines (writers) and are held to a higher standard of scrutiny. What I am recommending, to begin with, is a simple "storefront" of your own works. That is the best way to think of your online presence: as a storefront where readers and, even more importantly, potential employers or clients can sample your wares.

From getting work, to drumming up publicity, to gaining recognition, there are many advantages in going online with your résumé, clips, and more. Below, these are chrystallized into twenty-one reasons why the Net is one of the most powerful calling cards to the world.

Twenty-One Benefits of a Home Page

■ *REASON 1: A writer should have a virtual presence.*

You should go online for the simple reason that the Net is the place to be—it's the newest place, the most written about place, and the place receiving the most attention. More than just providing increased visibility, it is an unprecedented way to get vast exposure for you and your work to a potential audience of millions. While the entire global Netsurfing population—estimated at around 50 million—might not all drop in for a visit to your home page, many thousands, if not millions, just might.

■ *REASON 2: It's a way to make you and your writings available.*

Remember that no one can see your light (talent) if you hide it under a bushel. Putting your work up on a Web page makes it available to interested and potentially interested parties. Many artists and writers are temperamentally predisposed against the crass act of marketing themselves. In many ways, the Net is the perfect solution to this recalcitrance because it is unobtrusive—people only come to Web pages if they want to.

Remember to post all the basics about yourself as a writer, including key works that you have authored and contact information for those interested in retaining your services or publishing your writings.

■ *REASON 3: Making important contacts and sharing resources with fellow writers.*

In the same vein as the two previous reasons, having a home base on the Net allows for making contacts—"networking"—with a large pool of possible business associates who may want your services as a writer. And your page can act as a meeting place with other writers who share similar writing pursuits and who may also be willing to collaborate or share resources.

■ *REASON 4: Out and out publicity.*

Getting yourself written about in the news media helps to attract the attention of potential clients and of the public at large. And what better way to get the media interested than to have an interesting Web presence.

This is also helpful for the media because your home page can have answers to any of the possible "frequently asked questions" (FAQs) that could be queried about you. Think of a Web presence as your own small, public relations organization working for you full time.

■ *REASON 5: Whips up interest.*

You can use your home page to release material to the media and to the world at large in such a way as to increase traffic to your Web site. Much like sending out a press release, your page can have timely information placed on it—or recently completed writings—that could be of interest to readers. An example of this would be the publication of serialized material, with readers and news media waiting (hopefully) on the edge of their seats for the next installment.

■ *REASON 6: Sells your material.*

Once you have drummed up interest through Web marketing and publicity, perhaps now you can turn to the use of the Internet to actually gain remuneration for your work. Material that has an audience (i.e., reader interest) is of intrinsic value to the reader who may well be willing to pay something for access to that material. This can range from fiction writing to even more lucrative business writing.

The Net provides an economy of scale, whereby the purchaser pays only pennies because of the potentially large volume of readers for certain material via the Net. Thus, you could also think of your online presence as a point of possible commerce.

■ *REASON 7. Reaching like-minded souls.*

Inasmuch as the previous reasons cite your potential to reach an unprecedented number of people—particularly compared to other methods—you can broadcast and, at the same time, "narrowcast." The Internet, including the World Wide Web, is based on point-to-point transmission of material (people choose to access your material versus getting it "beamed" to them broadcast style like TV). As such, your material stands the possibility of getting accessed by the exact group that you want looking at it—whether mystery readers, financial news junkies, the education market, or whatever your specialty is.

■ *REASON 8. Keeping yourself in front of the public and staying in touch with loyal readers.*

Instead of the public saying, "Whatever happened to so and so, we used to read so much by him or her," now the public can drop into your "publication center" on the Web and see what you are up to.

In this same spirit, having your writings on the Web enables loyal readers to keep in touch with what you're up to no matter where they may be. For instance, in the case of newspaper writers, when a loyal reader leaves a newspaper's circulation area he or she need not lose contact with his or her favorite writers. The Net has a global reach and your writing is therefore "portable": material on your home page or with any cyberpublication can be read from any desktop in the world.

■ *REASON 9. You and your writing are available around the clock.*

While newsstands close, television broadcasts are limited in length, and other means of transmitting your material have time constraints, the Net never shuts down. In addition to giving you a global reach, any material or information that you have up on the Net is available twenty-four hours a day, which is of indisputable value. With the Web, you become an around-the-clock publishing service.

■ *REASON 10. Your material becomes quickly available and accessible in a timely fashion.*

Particularly for those writers who traffic in information about the financial world and markets, your time important information can go up on your Web page while it is still hot news.

Even with television, most information must wait until a broadcast goes on air. But with your important financial story, or anything else of a time-important nature, the Web provides a way to get it out instantly.

■ REASON 11. *Important information can be updated when needed.*
You can also update home pages to reflect changes in any expertise. The world is constantly changing, and the Net allows writers and their readers to keep up with these changes. This will become even more important in the quickly changing world of the future.

■ REASON 12. *With the Net you can get pictures and sound (i.e., multimedia).*
For the individual writer or publishing organization, or both, the Net provides a way to give readers more than just text.

You can have an entire print magazine, news broadcast, and radio program rolled into one with cyberpublishing. This makes the Net an attractive publishing opportunity because of the potential for creativity.

At just the simplest level of multimedia, imagine people reading your work, hearing it read by you, or, better yet, watching a video of you reading the material.

The list of possible multimedia bells and whistles goes on and should be seriously considered by writers approaching publishing in the new media.

■ REASON 13. *Getting response and feedback from your audience.*
Closely allied with several of the points made earlier about the Web as an entirely new technological means of publishing—boasting global reach and multimedia potential—is the often touted fact of its interactivity.

While the word *interactivity* has several meanings in the context of the Net and digital technology, most important to writers is the fact that readers can use your Web presence to give you feedback (via e-mail) about your work. Feedback allows one's reading public to communicate what they like or what they would like to see more of, and most writers find feedback both helpful to their work and, often, encouraging.

■ *REASON 14. The Net can act as your test market.*

Like getting feedback from loyal readers, having a section of your Web pages devoted to test runs enables you to get responses from visitors to your page—loyal or not—that may help you improve aspects of your work before it receives wider exposure.

Remember, as much as writers don't like criticism, a "word in season" from readers constructively suggesting changes can often save the day for a writer who may be heading his or her writing toward a cliff.

■ *REASON 15. Net publishing is inexpensive.*

Your most valuable time is that which you spend writing, and even vast technological changes such as those introduced by the Internet, cannot change the laborious art of writing.

But, inasmuch as you must spend the same amount of time (and time is money) authoring your news articles, short stories, novels, poetry, essays, or polemics, you can put these works on the Net at very little cost.

For the individual writer with an Internet account used for research and e-mail purposes, often the Internet service provider will offer several megabytes of home page space for free. Particularly when the space is free, you may as well fill it up—but not with junk. Your home page may prove to be the best selling tool that you have.

■ *REASON 16. The Net allows you to have value added for your readers.*

Whether you write about financial matters or author fiction pieces, there are some extras that you can give visitors to your Web page that you couldn't provide through other publishing means.

For instance, your page can act as a research toolkit for visitors by having a section that features links to the top five search engines or to several news services. Even more basic, you can feature references and links to Net-accessible material that may have relevance to the type of writing that appears on your page.

Many news-oriented Web sites—such as CNN or MSNBC—always have sidebar links to relevant URLs that accompany their stories. A story about crime may have a link to the FBI home page, or a story about Bosnia will have links to university sources that give a detailed history of that troubled region. You can also feature other specialized information services that give your readers some kind of added value for visiting your page.

■ *REASON 17. Save money on postage.*

Particularly if you are a freelancer, your virtual presence can act as your calling card to potential clients who can have instant and comprehensive access to your written works by browsing your home page. When responding to writerly help wanted ads or other leads, you can have possible employers drop in at your Internet address without mailing off an entire file cabinet of your work. This makes your Net presence a cost saver in the mailing department, which as many writers know, can add up.

■ *REASON 18. Your online presence as a virtual file cabinet.*

Net presence gives clients the chance to view an entire file cabinet worth of your previous work. This also means that your Net home page can act as a great archival source for you.

While you will always probably want to keep certain copies of your work on disk and in hard-copy form, having your best work on the Net means that you can go into your home page directory whenever you need an example of some of your better work to fax someone or for your own reference. This can save crucial time in looking through endless drawers or computer files, thinking, "Where did I leave that piece?"

■ *REASON 19. The Net, like a bookstore, is filled with literate persons.*

Most recent polling data shows that the Net is becoming equally used by women and men, that those using the Net have at least a bachelor's degree and earn a decent income, that users have eclectic interests, and that they love to read.

In short, Netsurfers are literate and literary. You could put a billboard on a busy highway advertising your latest essay on modern civilization and reach as many literate persons as happen to be driving down the road. On the information superhighway (excuse the term, but it's stuck), those cruising the Net are looking for something to read. They crave knowledge and, above all, information.

■ *REASON 20. The Net may actually replace TV.*

To put it euphemistically, we writers suffer from too much of a cash-flow crisis (we're poor) to have highway billboards, let alone TV commercials. The Net allows us an inexpensive "channel" with which to get our works into the public eye.

But even more key, writers use the Net because it is cheaper and still has broad reach. Some polling data shows that time spent on the Net is starting to replace that spent in front of the TV.

By using the Net, you may well be reaching people that can be reached only via the World Wide Web, and this includes people who use WEBTV because they are "watching" the Net and not television.

■ *REASON 21. Don't be a wallflower, join the party!*

We have established that by having a virtual presence, you can network and share resources with fellow writers, meet and greet clients for your work, drum up a readership and a following, and reach just the sort of people that you are looking for—people who read. Given this, even the toughest Luddite might want to think of the digital world of the Net as a useful tool, rather than as mere technology.

So, join the throng of your fellow writers as they "slip the surly bonds of earth," and exchange ink for digital ones and zeros in order to enter the ethereal world of cyberspace. In the next chapter: two writers who have.

■

Writers and Their Home Pages

et's look at how two writers are using the Internet to build their careers. The first, Hal Gordon, has
created a storefront Web site like that described in the previous chapter. The second, Tom Watson, took the route of using the Internet to
become a publisher, and, as the interview with him will make clear,
the venture has borne fruit for his writing career in all media.

Hal Gordon

Washington, D.C.–based writer Hal Gordon is a typical freelance
scribe. His writing portfolio is substantive and eclectic, with material
that ranges from speechwriting at the White House to ghosting several books. Gordon holds a law degree and his specialty is legal
affairs.

Gordon has written professionally for nearly the last two decades
and he knows all the tricks of the trade when it comes to securing
client leads, freelance assignments, and longer contract work. But,
recently, this "older dog" learned a new trick for marketing his skills—
he created a location on the Internet's World Wide Web that acts as
his calling card to potential clients the world over.

Let us open the curtain on the Hal Gordon home page and see what it reveals. Gordon learned how to publish on the Web as a term project while studying for a master's degree in communications at American University. Like many schools, American University has started to increase the offerings of new media classes in its curriculum. These include Internetology courses that Gordon and many others are rushing to study in order to stay current in their fields.

Gordon, who is like the majority of Netsurfers in having a simple dial-up connection to the Net, transferred the design work he had completed during his class onto a computer host area for private home pages that was provided free of charge by his Internet access provider.

The Hal Gordon Web site (*http://home.erols.com/gordonhc/*), entitled *The Friendly Ghostwriter*, opens with a simple page that advertises Gordon's ability to write anything from speeches to feature articles, annual reports, testimony, letters, and, now, Web pages for clients who need any or all of these services. In addition to listing these categories, Gordon also lists some brief reasons why ghostwriters or freelancers can help out an organization that needs writing expertise but has none on staff.

- Has your company's last downsizing left your public relations department understaffed and overworked?
- Do you need a top-notch speech, article, or writing project in a hurry?
- Do you want to look good in print or on the platform?
- No need to hire an agency or full-time writer . . .

Visitors to *The Friendly Ghostwriter* can click on a variety of sections, such as "My One Ghost Story" in order to view Gordon's résumé, "A Ghostly Voice" to see samples of his work, or a section that features a monthly column by Gordon. There is also a special section that deals specifically with legal writing—Gordon's specialty.

As a veteran freelancer, Gordon still uses traditional promotional methods—like large-scale mailings to potential clients—but he now combines his publicity notices with his home page. "I sent out one thousand postcards advertising my Web site to corporate PR departments across the country (any of whom may need a freelancer)," said Gordon of his promotional efforts soon after getting his home page up and running. He found that it is still quite a novelty to have one's own promotional Web site (remember, 80 percent of Americans aren't

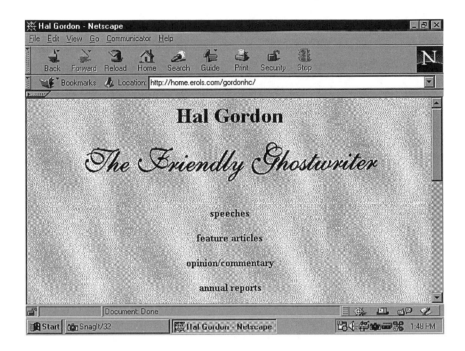

Hal Gordon is one of the growing throng of freelancers using the Net to drum up business.

even online yet). While talking to a client soon after launching *The Friendly Ghostwriter*, Gordon suggested looking up relevant material at his site.

"Oh," the client said with a hint of awe. "You have your own Web site?"

For Gordon, being this far ahead of the curve has advantages. "The Internet is still new enough and intimidating enough that having a Web site holds a certain cachet," he said. "If nothing else, it boosts my self-confidence to be able to tell potential clients that I'm on the Internet. Also, it is a lot easier to refer interested parties to a Web site than to mail out a résumé and a portfolio of writing samples."

Getting Your Home Page Noticed

Appearance is very important. Your site should be immediately inviting. There's no exact recipe for success, but we all know what's interesting when we see it.

ILLUSTRATION: Part of what makes a site interesting are the graphics used. Your site will be more alluring if it displays art that is illustrative and supportive of the text. Writing about birds? Then use some bird graphics, eggs, clouds, twigs. What about chirping sounds? Don't forget that the Web is a multimedia environment. Use the tricks to draw people into your writing.

INTERLINKS: This is the essence of the Net and its World Wide Web. Everything is interlinked with hypertext. Whether there are links between pages on your own Web site or links outside the site, there should be interlinking on your site (in fact, it's hard to avoid). Your outside links to the Net should support the material that is your content. If your page is about birds, you should have links to other bird pages (such as the Audubon Society).

An Interview with @NY's Tom Watson

There are 100 million stories in the digital metropolis that has been formed by the global Internet, and the story of Tom Watson is one of the better. Watson had the classic journalistic experience of pulling himself up by the bootstraps to reach the position of editor at a local newspaper in the Bronx (New York City.) But, as the Net and its glit-

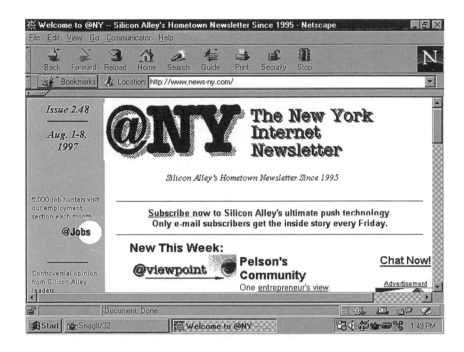

@NY, covering the waterfront of New York's "digeratti."

tery front man the World Wide Web began to grow in everyone's consciousness, he thought to cast his writing skills upon these new waters. His transition from stock-in-trade veteran journalist to a scribe in the new media has brought him from the ranks of being just another news writer laboring in the trenches to having a publication all his own—*@NY* Web magazine—and to writing on a larger stage in the still thriving world of hard-copy journalism with a regular column in the *New York Times.*

TKM: Tell us (fellow writers) a little about your writing background and the decision to begin publishing electronically—first with your e-newsletter and then your Web magazine, *@NY.*

Tom Watson: Well, here goes: I started out as a columnist in college for the *Columbia Daily Spectator* writing sports. Then I got a gig as a sportswriter for the Gannett Suburban Newspapers covering high school and college sports. After that, I became a reporter at the *Riverdale Press,* a top-notch weekly paper in the Bronx, and stayed there for a decade, rising to executive editor.

In the process, the paper was twice a Pulitzer Finalist and we won the First Amendment Award for not missing an issue after a terrorist firebombing destroyed the offices in an incident linked to Iran's death sentence on Salman Rushdie. I had the great experience of covering all the Bronx political scandals of the 1980s, and won more than a dozen national and state prizes for journalism. I got in the Net in 1994, like a lot of people, looking for information and trading e-mail. (Actually, I'd been using bulletin boards on and off for nearly a decade.)

During early 1995, Jason Chervokas—who was then the political reporter in my newsroom at the *Press*—and I started to look around for a way to get something going online. In the summer of 1995, fascinated by the new industry springing up in New York and the general buzz around town about the Net, we started formulating *@NY.* I posted to a couple of Newsgroups and lists, and before we wrote a word, we had more than three hundred subscribers. On September 1, 1995, we mailed our first issue—just two thousand words with a little news, some sites, and our general thoughts. It remained a biweekly until September, 1996, when we went weekly. The e-mail version now has more than four thousand weekly subscribers. We launched a small Web site in April, 1996, and redesigned it last fall. We get more than three thousand visitors a week, and the most popular section is the "@Jobs" area, where four thousand job hopefuls a month come calling.

In March, we were hired to write the new "Digital Metropolis" column for *CyberTimes*. A year later, we were named to write a new national column, "Digital Nation."

TKM: What are some lessons (triumphs and mistakes) you've learned in the last several years of online writing and publishing that you could impart to your fellow writers?

Watson: The lessons are simple: what people want online is information and the ability to communicate. We've succeeded because we've done both. But we haven't become rich by any means. We still make most of our money through freelance writing, and it can really be a grind. Two years is a long time to be independent Web publishers for a limited audience. Writing an e-mail newsletter puts a premium on length. We can't get too long-winded or people unsubscribe quickly. Most issues are around five thousand words. And we always answer e-mail to maintain a personal relationship with our readers.

TKM: What kind of opportunities does the world of new media make possible for writers?

Watson: It gives you the opportunity to own your own printing press. You may not make a bucket of money, but you can find your own audience without working for someone else. It also allows you to be close to the readers; something I learned in community journalism. Writing is valued on the Net—most of it (the Internet) is writing. So good writers have real value. It's also opened up the freelance market considerably for writers who know something about cyberspace.

TKM: In general, where do you see the world of online publishing currently and in the near future, and, more specifically, where does *@NY* fit into the scheme of things in the online publishing world?

Watson: Too much of what's written on the Internet is about the Internet. Of course, we're guilty as the next guy. I'd like to see more exploration of new ways of storytelling. In journalism, the Net is not a great place for the Hamiltonians among us—those who believe only an experienced journalist has a right to tell the story. It's too democratic, with millions of personal publishers. That's the real revolution. And that's where it will continue to grow. I saw stuff like "push technology" from the start as a desperate attempt to control distribution.

People who come from TV and print can't fathom not being in control of the distribution system. The Net, to them, is anarchy that must be controlled. I agree it's anarchy, but it shouldn't be controlled. There's no real need for a mining company to make sense on the Internet.

TKM: As a writer and a publisher, where do you imagine yourself and *@NY* to be in five and ten years? Do you have plans for "brand extension" or other new types of online publications? Any hard-copy spin-offs?

Watson: Yes, we have plans to take advantage of our small but valuable brand. We'll probably stay independent, but, in the world of covering technology, it pays to have a larger media partner to increase circulation and marketing. We'd also like to grow beyond the Net, both in coverage and, physically, in print.

TKM: Elaborating more on your thoughts about the *@NY* brand, what would you say is the scope of your coverage (i.e., beat), your editorial sensibilities, and the ongoing information goal of your online publication?

Watson: Good question. The scope of our coverage has changed and evolved from day one. At that point, we wanted to cover everything related to New York and the Net. In 1995, that was literally possible for two guys working part time. We knew and wrote about almost every story. Now, of course, it's impossible. We've become more narrowly focused to covering and analyzing New York's growing digital industry, with some spillover into real life (e.g., the arts, education, politics, neighborhoods, and preservation). But, even as an industry read—we call ourselves Silicon Alley's "Hometown Newsletter"—we're not lone voices anymore. There are literally dozens of reporters covering Silicon Alley now, and we started it. So, while there's a little satisfaction in knowing we were leaders, there's also a ton of competition for the news! That's why we try hard to analyze, to go deeper, to let our voices be heard. We have no desire to be another CNet or Bloomberg.

Still, *@NY* is a great brand. People remember it. We're even giving away some baseball hats with the logo on it, and many people want them. Our goal is to continue to have our voices be heard in the leading center of content production for the Net, and, in that way, to influence that development. Oh yeah, and to tell the truth.

TKM: You mentioned various freelance and other additional writing assignments that have been spurred by your visibility as creator and chief writer of *@NY*—such as your *New York Times* column and a book in the works. Could you tell me more about how online publishing has perhaps furthered your career as a writer?

Watson: Well, it's very simple: it's opened up a huge market that we walked into. I can remember working as a freelancer before the Net, and there weren't as many opportunities even in New York. The competition was fierce, but becoming an early Net guru was the ticket to the kinds of gigs I couldn't have gotten before. We've stayed independent thus far, but both of us have turned down full-time jobs paying $70,000—more than we would have expected to be offered a couple of years ago. And on the nitty-gritty side, the Web is a great research tool for writers, and e-mail is an incredibly powerful communications addition to the telephone.

You can read articles, columns, and other writings by Tom Watson at the following Internet addresses:

- *@NY*—The New York Internet Newsletter. "Silicon Alley's Hometown Newsletter since 1995." *http://www.news-ny.com*
- "Digital Nation"—Fridays in *CyberTimes*. *http://www.nytimes.com*.

■

Usenet Newsgroups and Listserv Mailing Lists

Some of the real interactivity of the Internet happens on the World Wide Web in the discussion groups that exist in mailing list Listservs and the Usenet Newsgroups.

Let us start with the Usenet and its nearly 20,000 Newsgroups, which aren't really about news at all, but exist to exchange information between people of similar interests and affinities. There are Newsgroups for topics from rocket science to rock music with everything in between, including many groups for writers and book lovers.

Newsgroups are e-mail–based forums. You can send e-mail messages to the group, asking questions, voicing opinions, or saying anything germane to the subject (at your own peril); other people in the group read the messages and respond to your questions or statements, or the messages that you post to a group can be a response to someone else's message. The continuum of responses and counterresponses to any particular message is known as a *thread*.

Participants in any one Newsgroup can come from anywhere in the world. The messages often reflect a wide range of experiences and opinions, often with stimulating people from around the world participating in a discussion.

Listserv mailing list groups are similar, but they are e-mailed directly to your Internet account (more about this later), whereas with the Newsgroups you must travel to the news server, where you need software known as a *newsreader* to access the group. Most Internet service providers (ISPs) also provide access to Newsgroups, with the exception of some groups that may be so marginal or offensive that the ISP will block access.

The Usenet, upon which the Newsgroups are hosted, was created during the Net's youngest days in the late 1970s. The Usenet and the few groups that were established back then were created to allow online meetings and discussions between computer programmers who wanted to exchange ideas, ask questions, or just chew the fat. Since that time, the number of Newsgroups has proliferated markedly, to say the least.

Newsgroup Organization

Newsgroups are given names that follow an established hierarchy designation, starting with the broadest category and then becoming more specific, with each category set apart by a period. The protocol *news:* precedes all Newsgroup names.

An example of interest to book lovers would be the following: *rec.arts.books*. The beginning category—the *rec.* part—is the official Usenet designation for anything recreational in nature, which is, of course, a broad category.

The other main groupings on the Usenet include the following:

- *comp*. For any topics that are computer related.
- *misc*. For topics that defy easy categorization—miscellaneous.
- *sci*. For (can you guess?) science-related topics.
- *soc*. For groups that focus on discussion of social issues.
- *talk*. For "talk" groups, in which participants can discuss a variety of topical material.
- *rec*. As mentioned above, this is for groups that are recreational in nature—anything from dog lovers to art to music and hobbies.
- *alt*. This domain is for "alternative" topics or those otherwise lacking the official sanction of a systems administrator or operator who normally presides over the operation of groups. The alt domain, despite its anarchic reputation, actually includes many middle-of-the-road discussion groups, such as *alt.civil.wars.usa*.

Given the eclectic and individual taste of writers, there are probably thousands of Newsgroups that might be of interest, but the following list includes just a few that deal with literary, journalistic, or other writerly areas. A comprehensive listing of both Newsgroups and Listservs is available courtesy the search engine Liszt (*http:\\www.liszt.com*).

Newsgroups

- *alt.journalism*. This Newsgroup is for journalists, journalism students, those marginally engaged in the practice of journalism, and assorted media hangers-on.
- *alt.journalism.freelance*. As the name implies, this group is for those journalists lucky (or unlucky) enough to be freelancers.
- *alt.prose*. A group covering all aspects of the art of prose.
- *alt.zines*. At one time the word *zine* was fairly obscure, but now these small operations often find themselves hitting the big time—particularly on the Net. This Newsgroup is dedicated to discussing the zine scene.
- *misc.writing*. This Newsgroup is for anyone from the beginning scribe to the accomplished stylist. This forum can be a good source of leads for places to submit work.
- *misc.writing.screenplays*. For accomplished and beginning screenwriters, this Newsgroup contains submissions, queries, information about markets, and the like.
- *rec.arts.prose*. This Newsgroup posts fiction for review and hosts discussion of posted articles.
- *rec.arts.poems*. The complement to rec.arts.prose, this Newsgroup provides posting and discussion of original poetry.
- *rec.arts.sf.written*. Looking to discuss science fiction? Look no further.

Listservs

Listserv mailing lists are also e-mail discussion groups composed of people interested in specific subjects or topics. Subscribers send messages to the Listserv address, and each message is automatically distributed to everyone who subscribes to the list.

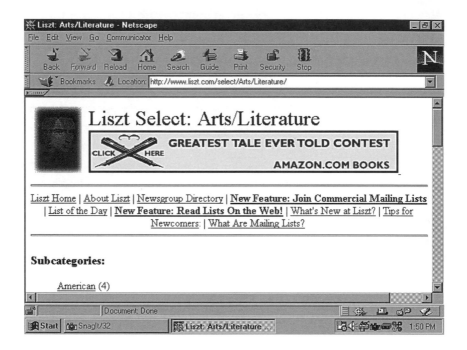

There are mere lists, and there is Liszt, a search engine that helps writers keep track of Newsgroups and Listservs.

Subscribing to Listservs requires that you have an e-mail address and a genuine interest in the topic of discussion on the list. If you subscribe to several active Listservs, you will find your e-mail box full of messages every day. If you find that the Listserv members are discussing items of little or no interest to you, simply send an e-mail cancelling your subscription to the Listserv.

Many Listservs are organized along professional lines. There are Listservs for accountants, lawyers, small-business proprietors, and journalists. To subscribe to a Listserv, you send an e-mail message addressed to the node (not the e-mail address) that manages the list, using the form: *listserv@hostname*. The body of the message should be in this form: "subscribe Listserv name [your first and last name]." For example, there is a Listserv dealing with computer-aided news reporting. Its name is CARR-L and the host name is *ulkyvm.louisville.edu*. To subscribe, you would send an e-mail to: *listserve@ulkyvm.louisville.edu*. The message on your e-mail should read: subscribe CARR-L [your first and last name].

A list of Listservs relevant to writers is given in the Appendix.

A Note on Netiquette

The word *netiquette* is simply an amalgam of *Net* (short for *Internet*) and *etiquette* (as in, how to behave appropriately). Netiquette is code of proper behavior on the Internet. The most basic rules of netiquette are those regarding the use of e-mail to the Usenet and to Listservs, and pertain essentially to writing or posting messages that don't reflect badly on you.

Remember that, while e-mail is private, it can be reposted with ease, so don't write anything you don't want reposted (i.e., don't send an e-mail to an officemate knocking the boss, because your co-worker might repost it to the wrong person, and get you in trouble). The same applies to love letters and other intimate missives—think twice about what you say and to whom you are sending it.

In the same vein that e-mail can be mislaid, as it were, it can become the focus of public scrutiny. Remember that on the Usenet and within Listservs you are in essence interacting in a public space. If you wouldn't shout something on a street corner, then don't do it in cyberspace either. Again, watch what you say, to whom you say it, and about whom you are saying it.

For most Usenet and Listserv postings, keep your messages short. Some folks insist on rewriting *War and Peace* on the Net. Considering the amount of e-mail everyone with Net access receives these days, it is rude to make people read overly long messages.

In this same spirit, keep your publicity/advertising efforts using e-mail, Usenet, and Listservs to a minimum. If you post overly obvious commercial messages—"Well-Made Decoy Ducks for Sale"—in the wrong places, you will be laughed at or, even worse, *flamed* (see Glossary).

As long as you stay within the boundaries of netiquette, Newsgroups and Listservs can be among the most freewheeling features of the Internet. They provide opportunities for keeping company with fellow writers and using that company to stimulate and test ideas. They can also be useful forums for informal networking and forging professional contacts.

■

6

Networking Through the Net

In this chapter, I discuss contacting publications and working with editors via e-mail, and mention some very important dos and don'ts. A list of addresses that will help you use the Internet for contacting publications is given in the Appendix.

Submitting Articles, Manuscripts, Drafts, and Queries

Anyone twenty-five years and older probably remembers perusing *Writers Market* and similar directories to obtain addresses of various publications and the names of relevant editors. You might print out a double-spaced manuscript with an individualized cover letter, slip it in a manila envelope, and address the envelope. After carefully preparing ten or twenty such packets, you might then trudge down to the post office and send them off at perhaps $1.25 a piece. Then the good part started. You waited for the rejection notices and, perhaps, one or two acceptances to arrive. Or you just simply waited, and nothing came in. Either way, it usually took weeks, if not months, to get a response.

Well, I won't say that thanks to the Internet and e-mail all this hassle has been eliminated—there are still circumstances that will require you to send hard-copy versions of your writing on speculation to editors—but now a great majority of your written liaisons with editors can be conducted via the Net, particularly through e-mail.

From the *New Yorker* to the *Washington Post* or the *San Jose Mercury News*, older mainstream media all have, at least, e-mail addresses where you can send "Letters to the Editors," and many also invite readers and writers to e-mail individual editors.

We emphasize, however, that when submitting material electronically, it be relevant to the publication. Remember, you don't like "junk mail" in your e-mail box, so don't flood others with items they might not find useful. Still, there's no harm in making e-mail cold calls—the worse that can happen is that an editor will delete your mail.

Again, the benefit of e-mail is that both parties save time and money compared to sending an initial query and manuscript via post. Also, besides having quicker turnaround time for initial inquiries, e-mail is exponentially faster than mail or fax for such things as revised drafts or completed manuscripts for which you have already been contracted for.

For freelance writers, the advent of e-mail has been nothing short of revolutionary. Writer Anthony Narcisso says that, "It's instant, it's efficient, and it's global. With e-mail, I just push a button and my correspondence flies to New York or Newfoundland, wherever the work is. E-mail has also taken the starch out of communicating professionally. Speed is highly valued these days, so the time-consuming formality of the hard copy business letter gets bumped in favor of a more casual tone." In particular, Narcisso notes the instantaneous turnaround he gains when responding to organizations advertising for writers.

While e-mail doesn't always eliminate the need to send hard-copy material, the combination of sending e-mail and so-called snail mail can work nicely to hook clients and publishers.

For freelancers, there is another distinct advantage to e-mailing material to potential employers or publishers: it shows that you are techno savvy and have taken the time and trouble to learn the intricacies of technological advances in the business world. And, for now, while many writers are still laboring with only hard-copy methods of reaching others, those writers who use the Net have an advantage.

In addition to the much older and existing media that now have provisions for submitting written works and queries electronically, one of the most potentially lucrative markets for writers is the newest of the new media, i.e., Web zines and the like.

This new breed of publication is the child, so to speak, of digital technology, and these Web publications take almost all their submissions via e-mail.

You will probably become familiar with these Web pubs and e-zines through some of the home pages that provide a hotlinked list of them, but you will also frequently see requests for submissions made by these publications within e-mail–based Usenet groups such as alt.prose or misc.writing. E-mail is enabling connections between writers and publications in both directions: writers are submitting work, and publications are posting help wanted ads using e-mail.

Again, using the Net and its e-mail facilities will not sell your material in and of itself, but if you are a craftsmanlike and professional writer (and we know you are), then using the Net can only help.

Contacting Editors: The Netiquette

In most e-mail contact with editors, it is best to first send a query with a short and to-the-point letter and a brief sample section of the piece you are peddling (versus the three-hundred-page manuscript itself).

As with hard-copy queries in the offline world, you should be familiar with the content guidelines and the general context of the publication upon whose door you are knocking (e.g., don't send *House and Garden* a story more suited to *Soldier of Fortune* magazine).

The key here is not to waste an editor's time, or your own, by submitting your work where it won't be appreciated. You never know when you may knock on an editor's door again, so don't burn your bridges by exploiting his or her time with too much e-mail and a lengthy, perhaps irrelevant, manuscript.

Requesting and following submission guidelines will help to keep you in editors' good graces. The guidelines are often available from the publication's Web site, and some of the e-mail directories (listed in the Appendix) include descriptions of the publications and submission guidelines. The following samples are from a directory called Bricolage at: *http://bel.avonibp.co.uk/bricolage/resources/lounge/TWRG/index.html*.

Writer's Nook News

Type: National quarterly magazine.

Content: Dedicated to giving freelance writers specific information for their immediate practical use in getting published and staying published. It contains news; writing tips; book reviews; legislative/tax updates; conference, contest, and market listings; and various related topics.

Compensation: The Nook News pays six cents per word on acceptance for First North American Serial Rights to short, pithy articles (400 words maximum) on the writing experience.

Comments: Simultaneous submissions will be rejected. Articles must be specific, terse, and contain information my readers can put to immediate, practical use. Avoid the third person whenever possible. Include a short bio (twenty-five words or so, not a résumé) with your submission.

Contact: Eugene Ortiz, publisher at *comprophet@delphi.com*.

Writer's Workshop Review

Type: Small Press Magazine (hard-copy), eighteen to twenty-two pages with plans to expand considerably. Began publishing in April 1993.

Content: How-to articles for writers, short stories in most genres, computer networking-related information, poetry, art, etc.

Compensation: Pays one contributor's copy. Editor plans to begin implementing program that will offer monetary payment.

Rights: First, one-time, or reprint rights. All rights revert to the author after publication.

Comments: We enjoy publishing a variety of different types of writing. We attempt to save as many of our pages for freelance work as possible, and we accept a good deal of work from unpublished authors. We encourage our writers to make every word count and to check over their manuscripts well to weed out weak sentences or ones with hard-to-understand phrasing. Most of our readers are computer users, and we advocate computer networking for writers. We encourage e-mail submissions and offer our guidelines via e-mail as well. We will send brochures to writing groups free of charge. We have a Bulletin Board Service (BBS) for writers on which we host Writer's Workshop, Writer's Workshop Lounge, and Writer's Garden (all VirtualNET Newsgroups, established in November 1992). Submissions may be uploaded directly to our BBS or sent through the Internet to the address below.

Contact: Editor, Rhia R. Drouillard at *inksling@workshop.rain.com.*

These two are just a small fraction of the various publications—small and large, electronic and otherwise—that accept electronic submission. To see the entire list, compiled by United Kingdom resident and Net literary expert Trevor Lawrence, go to the *Bricolage* Web site given above. A comprehensive list of e-mail addresses is also provided in this book's Appendix.

Cyber Help Wanted

A nother way the Net is changing the world of writing is in the field of good, old-fashioned job hunting. For writers, this doesn't mean finding just short-term assignments and writing contracts using the Net—but actual full-time positions.

What Color Is Your E-mail?

The Web has quickly become a top spot for general work-related searching, including going through the online classifieds that many newspapers host. It's handy to check habitually the many job-listing spots on the Web whether you are in desperate need of a job or "just browsing" for a change of pace. This is because of the many work possibilities that one can now access courtesy of digital technology. In fact, those who are not online yet run the risk of missing opportunities to those who find them first, posted online.

Prior to the Net and the creation of such Web-based work listings as the well-known Monster Board, job seekers were left with the option of searching help wanted advertisements in local papers or, perhaps, specialized trade journals.

Even with national trade journals, these hard-copy listings lacked the kind of geographical and work-function comprehensiveness made possible by the Net. Now, postings arrive on a variety of Web sites by the day, if not the hour, and they are searchable by a range of categories from geographical location to the type of work at which you excel.

The implications of job hunting via the Net are far-reaching. You will note that they are closely allied with the twenty-one reasons for writers to have an online presence.

■ *Internet Explosion.* With the rapid growth of the Net, the number of persons and organizations who are posting help wanted notices on the Net has also markedly increased. The explosion of employment listings on the Net is most likely on its way to making the World Wide Web the largest job-hunting market in the world. Also, many positions are now listed exclusively on the Net, so if you don't look here, you really will be left in the dark.

■ *Free Access to Premium Information.* In may ways, there is not more valuable information in the world for an individual than information on a decent job. We all must work for a living, but it helps if we can find a job that suits us and pays good money. The Net can help you find the right job, and most employment-hunting resources available on the Net are completely free of charge to job hunters.

■ *Free Dissemination of Information.* For those old-timers out there (over thirty), you may well remember copying hundreds of résumés, making many individual cover letters, compiling writing samples and tearsheets to mail out in hopes of hearing back a month latter. In almost one fell swoop, the Net allows you to post résumés and seamlessly send along work samples to hundreds of potential employers (all of whom are hiring), at the literal push of a button (a mouse to be specific).

■ *An Open Job Market Twenty-Four Hours a Day.* Often a job hunt can be limited by the nine-to-five routine. With the various job listings on the Net, you can look to your heart's content, and send along materials to potential employers, all after work.

■ *The World Is Your Oyster.* As previously mentioned, the scope of potential employment accessible via the Net is literally global. You will find listings of opportunities both close to home and elsewhere. If you are inclined to relocate, the Net can open that door for you, too. Plus, with the help of the Net, you can contact your prospective employer long-distance by communicating through e-mail.

Employment Surf's Up

The following listing of employment Web sites takes a look at some of the top spots, but is by no means a comprehensive collection of the job-hunting resources that exist on the Net. Particularly for writers, keep in mind individual newspaper, magazine, and Web publishers that may be of interest to you and relevant Newsgroups and Listservs that may occasionally carry job postings.

■ CareerPath.com: *http://careerpath.com*. One of the original comprehensive job-hunting Web sites, CareerPath.com is still one of the best. It posts an estimated 350,000 new jobs on its Net locale every month. It is updated daily with feeds from newspapers across the United States. Jobs listed here are searchable by job category, by keyword, or by the newspaper that initially listed the job. Also, CareerPath.com recently began featuring employer profiles where one can do research on "mini-home pages" that have the respective company information in which one might be interested.

■ Monster Board: *http://www1.monster.com/*. Monster Board is international in scope, but naturally one can narrow searches down to something more specific than just *the world*. And there are separate, smaller boards, such as Monster Board UK, which allow definitive searches in that particular country. American in origin, the Monster Board is most comprehensive when it comes to jobs in the good old U.S.A., where one can go from town to town looking at what's available or just key in writer and see what happens.

In addition to listing employment, the Board allows job hunters to post résumés to a central bulletin board. This essentially reverses the job-hunting process—not a bad thing—so that employers can find you when they're searching for staff. But, as most veteran job hunters on and off the Net will advise, don't just wait for potential employers to find you.

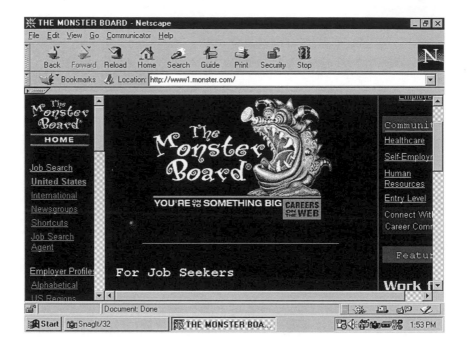

The Monster Board is one of several top-notch sites where you can search the world over for writerly work.

- CareerMosaic: *http://www.careermosaic.com/.* This Web site is another instance of the Net doing some of the hard work of job hunting for you because CareerMosaic builds a searchable database of résumés. Potential employers pay CareerMosaic for access to the résumés they host in order to find potential staff that fits their needs. You get to post your résumé for free. But don't just send in your résumé and forget about it; CareerMosaic will keep your résumé for only three months.

- America's Job Bank: *http://www.ajd.dni.us/.* This Net locale is hosted courtesy of the U.S. Labor Department and is paid for by Uncle Sam. Naturally, it lists jobs available only in the United States. But within that particular scope there is quite a bit to find. A recent check of America's Job Bank showed that there were 250,000 jobs listed, which means that the Job Bank has even more employment opportunities available than the more international Monster Board. And many observers have said that Job Bank has one of the more efficient search engines of any employment Web site.

   The Job Bank, however, lacks some of the extra features that one finds on some of the private services, such as allowing résumé postings and the kind of question-and-answer facility from job-hunting "experts" that some Web sites boast.

- College Grad Job Hunter: *http://www.collegegrad.com.* This site is, as its name implies, devoted to helping upcoming graduates find work. Quite simple in its operation, one just keys in a job category (*writer,* for instance) and the Job Hunter search engine will then list the names of companies with employment opportunities in that category.

   Also included at this site are helpful tips on résumés and cover letters, including advice on how to get your résumé passed around and noticed. There are even helpful tips about dressing for interviews.

■

Finding It on the Net

The ability to do research is one of the most important stock-in-trades that a writer or reporter can possess. For many writers, a large percentage of their work isn't just the writing they do, but the preliminary research on topics animal, vegetable, and mineral that feeds their ideas and enables them to write or reference knowledgeably.

You may be a novelist writing a medical thriller and you're looking for that perfect, obscure, jungle fever with which to kill a character. Maybe you're a murder mystery writer and you need to bone up on what kind of guns are currently being used by criminals. Or you could be a financial reporter and you want to track the stock performance of a certain company over the previous year. You might be a legal reporter on deadline who needs to double-check a recent Supreme Court decision about police search-and-seizure procedures. All this is "findable" (to coin a word) via the Net.

To do this, however, you have to cut through the jungle of information available on the Internet—the sheer volume of which is its strength, and its weakness. The Net is often referred to as the library without a card catalog, and, shopworn metaphor or not, it stands true that with over 100 million pages and counting on the World Wide Web alone, there is a lot to find—but it can sometimes take a certain diligence.

A writer, or any other type of researcher, begins an information search on the Net in one of three ways—through a directory resource, a search engine, or Web sites that deal with the specific topic of interest (such as going straight to the Library of Congress Web site to look up information on a bill).

Search engines are handy devices that spend a great deal of time "spidering" throughout the Internet and indexing the title, a summary, or indeed, in many cases, every word on Web pages and other Net documents (such as Usenet postings). This indexing allows the engine to collate relevant pages for information seekers, who can query the search engine with keywords (or phrases) that are related to the particular subject being researched.

The following is a rundown of the top Internet search engines currently available for helping researchers find their way through the Net.

Alta Vista

One of the most powerful search engines in use on the Internet is the Alta Vista engine, based on technology developed by the Digital Equipment Corporation. The promotional material for this engine says that it has literally millions of Web pages (21 million and counting) in its database, and from those sites billions and billions of words that have been indexed.

Many Net experts say that because this particular search engine knows every word on every page that it has indexed, it is the most comprehensive of the engines that are available. The fact that every word is indexed means that even if you are searching for a fact, figure, or other piece of arcana obscurely mentioned on a page, Alta Vista can help find what you are looking for. In comparison, many other engines index only portions of the Web pages through which they have spidered.

The flip side of the coin, some critics say, is that the results from using this engine tend to include the proverbial kitchen sink—almost any keyword that you might use will result in thousands of hits, most of which will prove to be dead ends.

With time, though, most Netsurfers learn methods to refine their searches so they are better able to find exactly what they are looking for. Still, in comparing the various engines, some veteran Netheads say that while Alta Vista is the most comprehensive, the other engines have better "relevance" rankings.

Alta Vista is searched by either a simple keyword or a string of words. Putting the words in quotation marks directs the engine to find only that exact occurrence of those words. And you can use what are known as Boolean operators—words such as *and, or, not,* and *near*—in order to refine your search by establishing a relationship between keywords. Alta Vista also contains a large-scale database of Usenet Newsgroups' (see chapter 5) messages that can be searched in a variety of ways.

Alta Vista is at this URL: *http://altavista.digital.com.*

Lycos

Like Alta Vista, the Lycos search engine also claims to have the largest indexed database of Web sites. Taking its name from the Latin word for spider, Lycos is one of the oldest of the spider programs that were created to crawl through the Net finding and indexing information.

Like Alta Vista, this engine can be praised for its comprehensiveness, but it also provides a large number of false hits. Lycos, unlike its rival engine Alta Vista, creates its database from spidering through the headers, the first paragraph, and the hotlinks on Web pages in order to index them. The results from a Lycos search are helpful in that the engine lists the number of times it finds your keyword on the indexed portion of a Web page, then snips out portions of the page with your keywords highlighted. Looking at these mini synopses is quite helpful in deciding whether to point and click on the link of the page that it found.

At this writing, Lycos does not allow the use of as many Boolean search operators as Alta Vista, but it promises to add more of these operators to help further refine searches.

Lycos can act as a hybrid between a search engine and a directory Web site (such as the famous Yahoo) because in addition to using keywords for a search throughout the Lycos database, there are subject categories from which one can choose to click on instead. Subjects include politics, government, computers, arts, literature, and humanities, and each has thousands of related URLs indexed for users to browse through.

Lycos is at this Net address: *http://www.lycos.com/.*

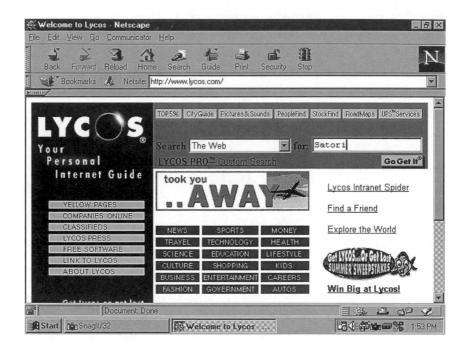

Among other search features at Lycos (Latin for spider*) is the City Guide where writers can glean information about cities around the globe.*

HotBot

Also in the running is the HotBot, which is a product of Inktomi Corporation and *Wired* magazine, a cutting-edge publication that reports on digital culture and technological invention. Given the origins of this engine, it has many features that some real Web experts thought would prove helpful in searches.

The HotBot has a database of around 60 million documents and can be searched by Boolean keyword methods (both simple and advanced). Similar to the relevancy rankings used by other engines, the HotBot will list its search results according to how often a keyword appears in the body of the document and also in the title portion of a document, which is the heading that appears at the top of a Web browser.

HotBot can also can be searched using a variety of "filters," which allow users to specify such things as the domain they want to search, or to limit the search to a particular geographical region. And one can search through the myriad Newsgroups on the Net using this engine as well.

Unlike some of the other search engines, HotBot does not offer any directory-like category breakdowns—such as government or arts and culture—though the staff of HotBot says there are plans to have such a resource soon.

To use the HotBot go to: *http://hotbot.com*.

InfoSeek Guide

The InfoSeek Guide engine does not claim to have the largest of the search engine databases, instead it asserts that it is the smartest and the fastest of the engines. The latter is hard to verify, but may be true.

Like its brethren among the search engines, InfoSeek is searchable by keyword. But it is different from many other engines in that you can enter a fairly sophisticated series of words, and instead of requiring you to put in various Boolean operators, the engine has a logic system that formats your inquiry behind the scenes. This frees you from having to learn to use the Boolean logic needed at many other engines.

With reference to the above "logic system," InfoSeek suggests phrasing your search in the form of questions, or as a request, such as "find me information on growing orchids indoors," and InfoSeek will go to work.

Like Alta Vista, the InfoSeek engine has indexed the entirety of the Web pages that make it onto its database. Its database, however, isn't as large as Alta Vista's.

Much like Lycos, the InfoSeek engine supplies helpful synopses of your search results. The synopses, some might say, are even better than Lycos in that InfoSeek lists the URL that it finds, the page title, and a computer-generated summary of what is on the page. It also provides the size of the file that it found, which is helpful in deciding whether or not to click on the result—if the result seems marginally relevant, you might not want to invest the time it would take to download a large file.

Like Lycos, the InfoSeek Guide has a directory section where Web sites are categorized topically—such as arts, entertainment, business, science, education, and politics.

In addition to having a searchable database of Web sites, one can use InfoSeek to troll through the Newsgroups in search of postings. For all searches, InfoSeek lists its findings in order of relevance to the keyword (or words) with which a user queries the engine.

InfoSeek also boasts a secondary service, by subscription, which specializes in searching through business-oriented databases.

To find out more about this and InfoSeek's main service go to: *http://guide.infoseek.com.*

Excite

Another top search engine is the Excite engine produced by the Architect Software Company. Excite distinguished itself early on by virtue of allowing not only simple keyword searches, but also by allowing concept searches. You could, for example, key in something such as "better living through healthier eating." Unbelievably, this actually works and such queries turn up relevant results in most cases.

Since this early innovation in natural language searching, at least one other engine, InfoSeek, has caught up with Excite by allowing a similar type of search. Nevertheless, Excite does a better job of explaining how to use concept search methodology and, on the whole, is simpler to use.

While not as voluminous as some of the other engines, the Excite database indexes the entire text of Web pages. Some reviewers have said that Excite maintains a more current database—important since the Web is constantly growing—and my experience with Excite concurs with this finding.

If you want to make sure you are finding the latest Web site pertaining to your particular interest, then Excite is the engine for you. And, like Lycos and InfoSeek, Excite also has a directory section where Web sites are categorized under topical headings. Making this doubly useful is Excite's staff of journalists on retainer who write reviews of various Web sites, which can prove very helpful. The results from searches with Excite are listed with a relevancy ranking, showing how closely each Web page corresponds to the keyword or concept search that you used.

Exicte can be found at: *http://www.excite.com.*

Open Text

Open Text, like several of the engines mentioned already, has a database with the entire text of Web pages documented. Recently, the size of its database soared from 1.5 million indexed pages to over 10 million pages, putting this engine in a league with Alta Vista and Lycos (which are always neck and neck for having the largest databases).

Search results are listed with a relevancy ranking and include the URL of the Web sites found, and Open Text supplies the file size of the Net documents that it has found.

This engine is laudable in that it provides for the most options in terms of search methodology. This includes the following: simple keyword searches using one or more terms; "power searching," which allows you to use up to five terms and Boolean operators between those terms; and you can create your own "weighted" search wherein you designate the relevancy of certain keywords that you want the engine to find in Web documents.

All these options cut both ways, however, as the advance searching can take a little practice and patience to learn. But once you get used to more advanced search capabilities, Open Text proves itself a very useful engine in terms of finding relevant and comprehensive results.

To use Open Test go to: *http://www.opentext.com.*

WebCrawler

The WebCrawler has a venerable history. About as old as Lycos, but unlike that engine and the others reviewed here, the WebCrawler opted to stay simple and "lean and mean" in its functionality. It doesn't come with the bells and whistles of many of its fellow engines, but its searches are quick and clean.

The results are listed with a relevancy ranking according to the keyword or words that you used, and the page title is listed. Lacking the synopses information that various other engines provide, with Web Crawler you are left with having to click on the pages found to browse through them for usefulness—that is, unless the title alone tells you whether a particular page is what you want.

Nevertheless, the pages that WebCrawler finds are often some of the most useful in that they are some of the more mainstream pages on the Net. This is because the Crawler's spider program hunts through the Net and compiles its database partially based on the popularity of pages. The pages indexed by WebCrawler are ones that receive a lot of hits. The usefulness of this, however, depends on what you are searching for. Because many pages don't make the cut, you won't get as many dead ends, but you also won't find more obscure data. The WebCrawler database only contains between 500,000 and 1 million Web pages.

To use WebCrawler turn your browser toward this URL: *http://webcrawler.com.*

Search engines are among the best tools for conducting research on the Net, and those described above are some of the top search engines currently plying the Internet. While many Netsurfers inevitably develop a fondness for one or two favorite engines, I suggest that, at least initially, you try them all out if only to learn more about the Net in general. Happy hunting!

■

9

Research Methodology

What are the research methods in a traditional library? You might go to the *Reader's Guide to Periodic Literature* or the card catalog, you may consult the reference librarian, or you may simply browse the stacks. Most information in a library is neatly broken down into categories—books, periodicals, audiovisual, archives—with categorized references available about where the information can be found. On the Internet, things are a little bit different.

When searching for the proper analogy, many people compare the Internet to a very large library. Still, others qualify this, saying it is a "library without a librarian" in order to take into account the inherently chaotic organization of the Internet. In doing research, it is best to understand that while the Internet is like a library, it cannot always replace a library.

The Internet is among the top methods for researching almost any subject. However, the Net should not serve as your exclusive method of research; it should serve as but one arrow in your entire quiver of research methods—traditional and otherwise. Put simply: You can find an enormous amount of information on the Internet, but you should also supplement that with a trip to a traditional library, depending on how thorough the scope of your research is.

Here are some thoughts on the Internet's research strengths:

- Good for access to government documents and publications that are either difficult to find or simply unavailable from a local library.
- Special online versions of traditional print materials—EDGAR (Securities and Exchange Commission company information), *Encyclopedia Britannica*, THOMAS (Library of Congress), Congressional Record, Electronic Newsstand—offering reprints of some (but not all) articles from major periodicals.
- Unique materials available only on the World Wide Web—software and shareware, electronic journals, and hypertext versions of periodicals that feature different content other than their traditional media counterparts.
- Press releases and media contacts—the Internet is a vast source of "unmediated" news.

Ten Tips for Internet Researching

Because one's expectation of the information superhighway can get easily overblown by hype and news media reports or by advertising that exaggerates the ease of Internet usage, you should keep a level head as you approach the Net. And, as in any other research endeavor, you should adopt a formal strategy to maximize results. Here are some tips that are commonly suggested for starting Internet research.

1. Ask yourself, your client, or your boss exactly what information is being looked for? Is it legal, scientific, literary, or artistic? Is the topic animal, vegetable, mineral? What is the subject category? Who may be the author? What is the date of publication? Is the material from a book, a magazine, a scientific paper, or an abstract? Are you looking for an electronic publication or a paper publication that may also exist in digital form on the Net.

2. While finding particular information on the Internet is exactly what you are trying to attempt, do you know that this information is somewhere on the Internet? Have you heard or read that it is on the Net? (As much as you can, find out where exactly it might reside on the Internet.) Did you previously run across a certain resource during earlier Internet research that you are now to trying track again?

3. What keyword or keywords might best help you find what you

The estimable archives of the U.S. Library of Congress are in the process of going online.

are looking for? This is especially needed when using Internet search engines.

4. As much as possible, familiarize yourself with what resources and organizations are on the Internet. There are a number of Internet-based and hard-copy directories that cite specific resources. When it comes to Internet-based directories, there are a number of top spots to begin your research. Yahoo (*http://www.yahoo.com/*), for instance, is still one of the premier Internet directory resources for beginning your research.

5. With regard to staying current in your subject area and aquainting yourself with what's out there, you should join relevant subject-related Listserv groups (mailing lists), and Usenet Newsgroups. As mentioned in chapter 5, there are thousands of them to pick from, covering every imaginable subject from biology to body piercing. There are a variety of electronic newsletters, such as Gleason Sackman's *Net Happenings Digest,* that publish new sites categorized by topic on a continual basis.

6. As you become accustomed to the Net, start "bookmarking" your favorite and most helpful home pages. The bookmark function is contained in all Web browsers and allows the Netsurfer to compile a list of Net addresses, so he or she can return to this list with point-and-click ease. For example, if you often research U.S. government information, you would want to bookmark THOMAS, the Internet guide to the government hosted by the Library of Congress. (*http://thomas. loc.gov*)

7. After you have familiarized yourself with the many informational resources on the Internet and have become knowledgeable about all the different Internet guides and search engines, you should maintain a high degree of discipline while researching. Remember to stick to the topic you are looking for. With an estimated 100 million pages on the World Wide Web portion of the Internet alone, it is easy to find yourself sidetracked as you are led down the garden path away from your original topic. The Internet is Victorian in its eclecticism, and that is both its beauty and its danger. So stay focused and don't wander from Civil War history into the War of the Roses when you stumble into a university history department somewhere on the Internet. (This abundance of informational resources was coined "future shock" by writer Alvin Toffler in 1965.)

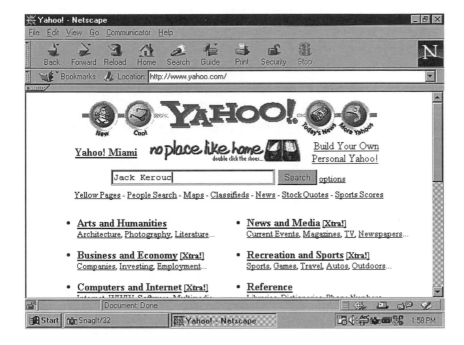

Named after the creatures in Gulliver's Travels, *Yahoo is the single best topical guide to the Net.*

8. Closely related to the need for discipline is the continual willingness to scrap your initial Internet research findings and to use different keywords or take a look at other Web sites if those you are browsing are not yielding good results. Let's say, for example, you are looking for cultural information on gay events, happenings, and writings: do you use the word *gay* or *homosexual* as a keyword? With the word *homosexual,* you are likely to run across information of a more scientific nature than if you had used *gay.* If the initial information you find is a red herring, then go back and start again. Also, if you have passed by a home page that seemed more relevant to your research, use the "back" arrow function on your Web browser to go back and look at that page.

9. What happens when you can't find the answer to your research question? First, look at your resources. Are they appropriate to your search needs? For example, are you trying to search for a piece of legislation that contains the word *communications?* If you use any of the larger search engines for this keyword, you will get thousands more hits than you want. Instead, go to a specific Internet resource related to the subject (e.g., legislation) such as THOMAS at the Library of Congress.

In general, as you begin your research, try to find the most appropriate resource related to your query. In a traditional library, you wouldn't use a periodical index to look for books. Using the right resource holds equally true on and off the Net.

10. How do you know when you have successfully concluded your research on the Internet? This can be problematic in part because of the large scale of information available on the Internet. Often, however, you know that your search is over when you have answered the question you first posed: What are the opening lines of the Gettysburg Address? What year did Columbus discover America? What did the Supreme Court decide regarding abortion in *Roe v. Wade?* In Internet research, as in other mediums, the complexity of the answer you are after will depend on that of the question initially posed.

■

Searching for Shakespeare— A Case Study

et's trace the steps of a rather simple example of Internet research, but one that reveals the typically winding path encountered as one searches for information on the Net. As the ides of March approached, I set out to find the well-known quotation, "Beware the ides of March," from Shakespeare's play *Julius Caesar.*

I began my hunt on the Excite search engine (*http://www.excite.com*) by entering *ides of March* and *Shakespeare* under the concept-search heading. Although I was looking for the Bard's *Julius Caesar*, it took some hunting through various other Shakespeare-related resources before I actually found a firm lead to *ides*. The fact is that devotees of William Shakespeare have woven a rich tapestry of plays, scholarly discussions, and Shakespeare arcana on the Web.

Several Web sites proved dead ends, but one ultimately led me to the passage I sought. The site is called Mr. William Shakespeare and the Internet (*http://www.palomar.edu/Library/shake.htm*), and is one of the single best sites for studying and quoting the Bard. This relatively new site has pledged itself to the purpose of listing the many informational links to Shakespeare text, criticism, and education. Also available from the Mr. William Shakespeare page are links to Elizabethan and Renaissance resources.

Terry Gray, the author of this excellent page, has annotated the links with personal commentary, which is helpful as you navigate through the site in search of a particular morsel of information. In an opening message, Gray says, "If you are a true Shakespearean, the term *scholarly material* will translate as *fun*. If you are being forced to take a Shakespeare class or do research, this is your chance to become a true Shakespearean and develop a love and enjoyment for the best poet ever."

Once there, some of the key links to other Web sites include: Bartlett's Famous Shakespeare Quotations, a searchable index of Shakespearean sonnets and other poetry, and a searchable index of all Shakespearean work. There is also a link to answers for questions frequently asked about the man, and a link to the Shakespeare Illustrated site, which features a variety of nineteenth-century oil paintings depicting scenes from the Bard's works. Under the Renaissance category, there is a guide to proper Elizabethan pronunciations and access to a number of musical sites with sound files of Renaissance-era music.

The available scholarly criticism of Shakespeare includes the writings of fellow Englishman Dr. Johnson and a link to the Richard III Society, where one can read a tract by scholar James A. Moore, entitled "Historicity in Shakespeare's *Richard III*" (*http://www.webcom. com/~blanchrd/bookcase/moore1.html*). This particular passage, which examines Shakespeare's possible role as a Tudor propagandist, caught my attention, and, despite my advice in the previous chapter urging researchers not to get distracted, I let myself be led temporarily astray.

"Throughout the twentieth century, historians and literary critics have thoroughly understood the Tudor bias tainting the historicity of Shakespeare's sources for *Richard III*, found not only in Thomas Moore's *History of Richard III*, but especially in the chronicles of Polydore Vergil, Edward Hall, and Raphael Holinshead," writes Moore. "Cursory examination of statements about Shakespeare in *The Ricardian* reveals a healthy respect for his genius. Seldom have they accused him, with Thomas Moore and the Tudor chroniclers, of being a deliberate propagandist for the Tudors. Furthermore, reviews of *Richard III* stage productions generally have focused upon dramatic merit rather than strictly upon historical deficiencies."

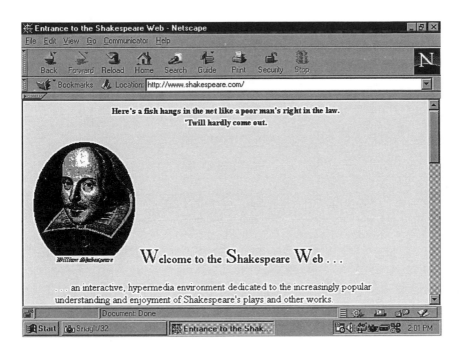

The "Immortal Bard," Mr. William Shakespeare, lives on via the Internet.

Curiosity satisfied, I returned to my quest for the *ides of March*. I traveled, via a link, from the Mr. William Shakespeare page to one of the most interesting search engines on the Net—the Shakespeare Search page at the Massachusetts Institute of Technology (*http://the-tech.mit.edu/cgi-bin/shake-search.pl*).

The Shakespeare Search page is one of a number of "mini-search engines"—known as Wide Area Information Searchers (or Servers), WAIS for short—that actually predate the current crop of powerful engines such as Alta Vista or Lycos, which search and index the entirety of the Web. Courtesy of the WAIS, I was able to quickly find references to *ides*.

In fact, I not only found seven references to *ides*, but the entirety of Shakespeare's *Julius Caesar*. Indeed, MIT has the entire texts of Shakespeare available online.

I clicked on the first reference and was taken to Act I, Scene 2, of *Julius Caesar:*

> *Flourish.*
>
> *Enter Caesar, Antony, for the course; Calpurnia, Portia, Decius Brutus, Cicero, Brutus, Cassius, and Casca; a great crowd following, among them a Soothsayer.*
>
> CAESAR: Set on; and leave no ceremony out.   *Flourish.*
>
> SOOTHSAYER: Caesar!
>
> CAESAR: Ha! who calls?
>
> CASCA: Bid every noise be still, peace yet again.
>
> CAESAR: Who is it in the press that calls on me? I hear a tongue, shriller
> than all the music. Cry Caesar! Speak, Caesar is turned to hear.
>
> SOOTHAYER: Beware the ides of March.
>
> CAESAR: What man is that?
>
> BRUTUS: A soothsayer bids you beware the ides of March.
>
> (Found at: *http://the-tech.mit.edu/Shakespeare/Tragedy/juliuscaesar/juliuscaesar.1.2.html*).

If I had known, I could have gone directly to MIT's Complete Works of William Shakespeare home page (*http://the-tech.mit.edu/Shakespeare/works.html*), which allows one to click on a play by title under the neatly categorized sections of comedy, history, tragedy, and poetry.

When I began my search for the quote, the Excite search engine led me to several interesting Shakespeare sites. The Shakespeare Oxford Society (*http://www.shakespeare-oxford.com/*) lists a solid compilation of Bard links and is devoted to the pursuit of questioning Shakespeare's authorship of the plays and sonnets he is credited with writing. The opening message from the Society's home page reads: "The purpose of the Shakespeare Oxford Society is to document and establish Edward de Vere, seventeenth Earl of Oxford (1550–1604), as the universally recognized author of the works of William Shakespeare."

The mainstay of the Society's publishing effort is its quarterly *Shakespeare Oxford Newsletter* (curious, considering its members don't think Shakespeare is actually Shakespeare), a hard-copy missive, and the *De Vere Reader*. The latter is an online magazine that carries articles, news, debates, and bibliographies which "impart a wide range of corroborating information and commentary," regarding Edward de Vere's true right to the Bardic title. Also at this site is a Beginner's Guide to the Shakespeare Authorship Problem. But let's not get tangled in this debate. The following are some other top Shakespeare sites:

The Shakespeare Web (*http://www.shakespeare.com*) is a solid site, particularly with regard to its Queries and Replies section about the Bard. But one gets the impression that the site hasn't been maintained much since an ambitious launch last year. The site includes listings of Shakespeare's theatrical productions and festivals across the country.

The Shakespeare Web site not only recommends MIT's Shakespeare search engine but also gives thumbs up to a search site (and entire text) maintained by James Matthew Farrow of Sydney University's Basser Department of Computer Science (*http://www.gh.cs.usyd.edu.au/~matty/Shakespeare/*).

■

Tune Up Your Writing

There are clearly many opportunities in the new media for writers. And experienced writers don't have to be intimidated because the Internet is a new venue for them. Writing is writing, regardless of where it appears. However, writers new to the Internet need to keep in mind that readers can exit their prose in a flash, or rather in the click of a mouse. What makes the Internet and its World Wide Web so fascinating and easy to navigate, also constitutes a slippery slope for writers. More so than in any other medium, writing on the Web must be interesting and compelling. Once it gets dull, the reader may click the mouse and say good-bye.

Online Education

Throughout this book, I assume that most readers are already competent writers. But if you think your writing can stand some brushing up before venturing into cyberspace, there are ample opportunities to get some first-rate tutoring on the Internet. This comes in the form of distance learning, virtual classrooms, and online writing labs (OWLs).

One of the great traditions of writing is that knowledge is passed down from professor to student, from master writer to apprentice, or from mentor to tutee. Almost all writers can cite a particular class or person who helped shape their writing from diamond-in-the-rough to sparkling prose. This grand tradition continues on the Net, where it melds with another tried-and-true educational institution—the correspondence school. Online, it's known as "distance learning."

All across the academic landscape, writing students are attending classes, getting assignments and critiques, working with professors and fellow students, and, ultimately, receiving grades—online. And while it is doubtful that physical campuses will ever disappear in favor of the cyberclassroom, there is a growing trend afoot at most universities to offer virtual degree programs entirely online. Also, a number of states are examining the creation of entire virtual universities, which will have no campus at all. These will not be fly-by-night academies and shady degree programs; the plans are for fully accredited institutions.

The Net has ushered in a new era of education that can be of great benefit to all manner of scholars, including writers and potential writers, who want (or need) instruction but may not be able, due to distance or time constraints, to attend the institution or class of their choice. Distance learning offers writers the opportunity not only to brush up their literary or journalistic skills, but also to explore new subjects and find information that can be used in their writing.

"We're starting to see a revolution" Nick Allen, the dean of Maryland's University College, told *Washington Post* reporter Rene Sanchez. "These are real classes and real degrees only a modem away." What the Net replaces is the clunkier practice (though it had its place in history) of the correspondence school, where professor and student mailed assignments, critiques, examinations, and evaluations back and forth via the postal service. Now, with the expected ubiquity and efficiency of electronic and digital communications, the once small niche that distance learning occupied is starting to expand dramatically.

The form that these online classes take is varied. In some "virtual classes," the professor posts lecture notes and assignments to a central electronic bulletin board accessible to the virtual students. Students then use e-mail to ask questions to their professors and deliver finished assignments for grading.

Other types of distance learning make even more progressive use of the Net by using *chat room* technology (see Glossary) in order to have full-class meetings, in real time, all online. This allows for symposium-style discussion and group work on assignments.

Then there are the virtual reality experiments through which students gather within the same classroom in cyberspace. No doubt that with the further perfection of virtual reality technology, distance learning will evolve so that the students and their respective professors, though all geographically separated, will seamlessly meet to discuss and debate within a virtual classroom that recreates much of the atmosphere and interactions that we associate with attending school.

For those who would like to read and study further about the growing practice of distance education, the University of Wisconsin has created a Web guide and clearinghouse on the topic: *http://www.uwex.edu/disted/home.html*. Also helpful is the Distance Learning Resource Network: *http://www.fwl.org.edtech/dlrn.html*.

Online Writing Labs

Whatever form distance learning takes, there are already many opportunities for writers to take online classes, either in entire online programs or in single accredited courses.

Some of the earliest, and most quickly growing, manifestations of distance education are the myriad OWLs that have been created, or are being created, by hundreds of schools. These are the natural technological extension of writers' workshops and individual tutorials that have existed for years on the campuses of many schools.

One such writing lab is hosted by Purdue University at this Net address: *http://owl.english.purdue.edu*. Dr. Muriel Harris, a founder of the Purdue OWL, describes, on her personal home page, her school's online writing lab and how it can benefit both Purdue student writers and writers at large. "My interest in getting OWL to fly is that I want our writing lab to offer Purdue students (and others out there on the Internet), a desktop writing tool. OWL is a way to have easy access to our files of homemade instructional handouts, to contact us with questions, or to talk about writing. I see OWL as a logical growth in our writing lab services."

A quick review of OWLs on the Net shows that Dr. Harris's com-

Online writing labs are part of the shape of things to come for the "virtual classroom."

ments stand true to the function and purpose of many OWLs. To varying degrees, each OWL offers some of the following:

- a conduit for communication between writing tutor and tutee
- a means of distributing learning resources (topical handouts) to student writers
- a collaboration between students and an opportunity for group critiques
- a meeting place of like minds and talents
- a showcase for student works and publications
- a jumping-off point for research into the greater Internet

A selection of OWLs:

- Bowling Green State University OWL "Writime." *http://www. bgsu.edu/departments/writing-lab/Homepage.html*
- The Dakota State University OWL. *http://www.dsu.edu/departments/liberal/owl*
- The University of Maine "Writing Center Online." *http://kramer. ume.maine.edu/~wcenter*
- The University of Michigan OWL. *http://www.las.umich.edu/edb/ OWL/owl.html*
- The University of Missouri's "Online Writer." *http://www. missouri.edu/~wleric/writery.html*
- Rensselaer OWL. *http://www.rpi.edu/dept/llc/writecenter/web/ home.html*
- MetaIndex of OWLs at the National Writing Centers Association (based at Colgate University). *http://www2.colgate.edu/diw/ NWCAOWLS.html*. The MetaIndex, courtesy of Bruce Pegg at Colgate University, allows you to scroll through hundreds of hypertext links to various OWLs and writing centers. The list is searchable alphabetically by school. Also hosted here is a large list of general resources available on the Internet for writers.

For Rebecca Rickly, OWL coordinator for the University of Michigan, the online tutoring made possible by the Net allows beneficial tutoring of U.of M. students and the educational community at large. "While OWL is still evolving here, we're excited about the future. We see it as the center of a variety of other projects," she writes. "For instance, we'd like to begin a cyber mentoring program with an inner-city Detroit high school, where Michigan (U.of M.) peer tutors establish an in-depth, one-on-one relationship with high school students, helping them not only with their writing, but introducing them to academic life from an insider's point of view."

Handouts

Besides providing an opportunity for registered student writers to attend long-distance classes, many OWLs offer freebies in the form of "handouts," which include writing tips and tutorials that are made available to all interested parties at their respective Web sites. The following excerpt from a handout archived at the University of Ohio OWL is just a brief example of the thousands of writing tip handouts that have been made freely available by many of the OWLs.

ON STATING A THEME IN LITERATURE

1. Theme must be expressible in the form of a statement with a subject and a predicate. It is insufficient to say that the theme of a story is motherhood or loyalty of country. These are simply the subjects. Theme must be a statement about the story's or poem's subject. If we express the theme in the form of a phrase, the phrase must be convertible to sentence form. A phrase such as "the futility of envy," for instance, may be converted to the statement "Envy is futile": it may, therefore, serve as a statement of theme.

2. The theme must be stated as a generalization about life. In stating themes we do not use the names of the characters in the narrative, for to do so is to make a specific rather than a. . . .

(Found at: *http://www.lima.ohio-state.edu/~WACC/WC-Handouts/lit-theme.txt*).

A further list of handouts at the Ohio State site includes how-to information on researching papers, guides to spelling, guides to rewriting and proofreading, a guide to résumé writing, and a guide to writing introductory paragraphs.

Educators who advocate the benefits of distance learning—and they seem to be growing in number—say that in addition to giving greater access to college courses, in general, these courses are inherently less expensive. Not as ivy covered as the traditional campus, virtual schools are at least not beset with the problems of building maintenance and overhead.

■

Book Marketing and Sales

The Internet, especially the World Wide Web, has quickly grown into a viable medium for both the selling and marketing of books. In this chapter, we take a look at one of the top spots on the Net for book sales, a Web site that features an epic amount of titles: *Amazon.com*. The great success of Amazon has drawn other giant booksellers to the Internet, most notably Barnes and Noble.

We also will drop in at some smaller, equally important operations that allow browsing of the stacks and ordering via the Net—bookstores that are, in short, using the Internet to conduct business, whether locally or globally.

Amazon.com

"If it's in print, it's in stock!" is the Amazon.com motto, and the Amazon.com bookstore on the Internet claims to be the largest bookstore in the world. Like the famous South American river after which it is named, this literary venture is indeed immense. Go to the Amazon site on the World Wide Web (*http://www.amazon.com*), and the opening Web page will tell you that there are at least a million titles available through this online ordering service. There is little reason

In many senses of the word, Amazon.com can lay claim to being the world's largest bookstore.

to dispute the claim—in fact, it's hard to find a book that you can't order through Amazon.com.

To Jeff Bezos, founder, operator, and CEO of the world's largest bookstore, a virtual bookstore was the realization of a long-held ambition. "I've always been interested in industries that are not just being changed by computers, but industries being revolutionized by computers," said Bezos in a news interview shortly after the 1995 launch of this venture.

And how! The old media have become new media via the Internet, and the venerable old art of bookselling is indeed also being rapidly changed by the Net. Bookselling is a business that is particularly amenable to going online. In part, this is because operations such as Amazon.com are able to deliver solid customer service and offer a vast inventory of books with a lower overhead.

Imagine the physical resources an actual bookstore would require to house a million titles. According to one estimate, Amazon.com stocks more than seven times the number of books that might be on the shelves of even the largest Barnes and Noble bookstore. Amazon has its books warehoused near its headquarters in Seattle. The online storefront is supported by a huge central shipping operation.

Adding to Amazon's appeal are its discounted prices. The discounts grew much larger when other giant booksellers ventured onto the Net and gave them competition. Shortly after Barnes and Noble "opened up" on the World Wide Web, Amazon began to offer 30–40 percent discounts on some titles.

Nevertheless, Bezos says that his aim isn't to replace physical bookstores in the offline world. "We're not going to replace the bookstore," Bezos told *WebWeek* reporter Jeremy Carl at the time of Amazon's launch. "One of the things that's interesting about books as a product is that people go to bookstores in part because they want books, and in part because they want a nice place to go. It's a challenge for all interactive bookstores to make their [Web] site as engaging as possible."

To accomplish this, Amazon has interactive features. Customers submit their own book reviews and there are reading groups and real-time discussions with authors via the Net.

And there is Amazon's greatest feature—its online searchability. The entire catalog of more than a million titles is searchable by author, subject, title, and keyword. You can chose a book by perusing

Amazon's recommended reading list, or you can look for books under sectional headings, such as computers or novels. There is also a personal notification service, which is becoming typical of online businesses, whereby e-mail is sent to you when a particular book or books related to your topic of interest are available.

Foremost, Amazon is a successful paradigm of conducting business on the Web because bookseller and book purchaser actually transact their business on the Web site. This is unlike many business Web sites that provide inventory and ordering information but aren't equipped to sell their product via the Web.

Delivery is promised within seven to ten days, and Amazon will even gift wrap books ($2 extra). Of course, people are still learning that they can buy items online and getting over their fear of credit card pilferage via the Net. Once they do, it should be somewhat like the catalog sales boom that started a few years back—such as J. Crew or Land's End—where buyers quickly adopted the habit of ordering with a credit card on the phone.

Bezos says that the art of online sales is in its relative infancy and that buyers still need to learn "a whole new set of habits." And he advises that any business venture entering new sales territory like the Web must be prepared for the long haul. "The landscape of people who do new things and expect them to be profitable quickly is littered with corpses," Bezos warns.

The Independent Market

The Net is often said to be a "level playing field" because all Web sites are potentially equal, and, so, smaller independent bookstores are also using Web marketing to leverage their relative market position and sales levels. Put more simply: the Net allows them to increase the amount of sales above and beyond what they sell to their walk-in trade.

While there are literally thousands of examples of independent bookstores that have some kind of Web presence, let's look at how two bookstores are publicizing themselves and marketing books via the Net.

Booksmith

"Welcome to Booksmith, San Francisco's leading independent book-store," reads the opening message on the Booksmith home page. "We're more than just a virtual business, we're more than just a bland chain—we're a real bookstore with an experienced, friendly, and knowledge-able staff." This nice, warm hello from Booksmith bookstore in the Haight Ashbury District of San Francisco let's you know what the store is all about, and that it is staffed with real live human beings. Keep reading and you will also learn that Booksmith has been open for more than twenty years.

Getting down to brass tacks, the Booksmith home page has a searchable inventory of more than 50,000 on-hand books, audiotapes, calendars, and CD-ROMs. You can look for any of these items by au-thor or title, or you can just browse through what's available in the inventory by topical category or at random to see if anything strikes your fancy. The official categories of merchandise available include: fiction, nonfiction, children's books, multimedia, science fiction, and a category intriguingly called "Spin the Dial."

There is also a listing of books that are on sale, which the Web site tells us are discounted anywhere from 40 to 90 percent. This list is frequently updated or changed, according to what's in stock. And there is a listing on the home page for books autographed by the author, plus a listing of collectible books.

Other information dispensed by the page that may be useful to writers located near the store, or planning a visit to the vicinity, in-cludes a calendar of book signings and poetry readings. As of this writing, Booksmith provides a toll-free number to order books rather than online ordering.

For an online sojourn into the Booksmith store, go to: *http:// www.booksmith.com.*

The Midnight Special

Located in Santa Monica on the Third Street Promenade, the Midnight Special Bookstore is another independent West Coast bookstore that has placed some of its business online. According to the About the Store statement on its home page, this is a store with a mission: "Midnight Special is a social and cultural bookstore presenting books and ideas to change the world."

That aside (what independent bookstore doesn't want to change the world?), the store has converted each of its physical sections into Web pages, with each page supplying its own resident expert, who answers inquiries on the topic at hand. In total, Midnight Special has nearly 100,000 titles in stock, any of which can be searched and ordered via its Web site.

Also at the Midnight Special Web Site are book reviews and staff recommendations of various books, and, like the Booksmith home page, there is a calendar of events at the store. The events range from topical seminars and author readings to poetry slams and even Internet tutorials.

Of particular interest to some Netsurfers might be Midnight Special's Opinion section wherein the store as a group entity expresses its opinion "on the affairs of the day," and, in turn, invites responses to these opinions.

To drop in at Midnight Special, visit: *http://labridge.com/msbooks/homepage.html.*

∎

E-zines and Other Writerly Spots

Gregg Micklos

First there was the printing press, then came the Internet. The world of home pages, e-mail, e-zines, and Web magazines has been a welcome invention for novice and professional writers. Never before has a writer, regardless of the message or ability, been able to publish to a worldwide audience as easily as he or she can today on the Internet.

Many editors of Web magazines and e-zines say the Internet has conventional publishing a little on the edge. "Never before has the literary elite so lacked control," says *Urban Desires* editor-in-chief Gabrielle Shannon. The Internet has made it possible for anyone to publish his or her work on the World Wide Web, either by going through an established Web magazine, an e-zine, or by creating his or her own home page.

But with the new opportunity comes a challenge. Writers now have to promote their own work, which some experts say can be a very difficult process. Some readers also complain that the quality of writing on the Internet is generally lower than that of conventionally published material. "Because it's so easy to put something out, people allow themselves to get sloppy," says Web editor Bob Biderman.

Many writers and editors currently publishing on the Web are cautiously optimistic about the future. They are concerned about the imminent influence of the corporate world. Also, they say, many e-zines will probably die because of the human effort necessary to maintain them.

But no one knows for sure. Web magazines like *Salon*, *Urban Desires*, and *Slate* might be the way of the future, and as more people get on the Internet, more writers will be looking for an inexpensive way to expose their work to this vast, worldwide audience.

E-zine List

In the 1960s, many writers published their work in small publications called *zines*. These were generally sold in small bookstores, especially in the major cities. In the 1990s, zines reemerged, first as hard-copy publications and then, with the arrival of the Internet, in electronic versions on the World Wide Web. The Web has thousands of e-zines, usually produced by one person or a small group of people. The best way to find these e-zines is to visit the *E-zine List* (*http://www.meer.net*), a Web site—created by John Labovitz in the summer of 1993—that lists, describes, and links thousands of e-zines on the World Wide Web.

"It seemed like there was a need for a more organized directory that kept track of where e-zines could be found, so I grabbed the relevant information from a couple dozen e-zines and created the first version of the E-zine List," explains Labovitz. Today, the E-zine List has links to close to one thousand e-zines. Labovitz says he adds, on average, one new e-zine submission every other day.

But are these the best e-zines on the list? According to Labovitz, "I don't try to judge the e-zines, I just list them." He says e-zines come in all different shapes and forms and that's the fun part of it. They are often produced for fun or personal reasons. "[They] tend to be irreverent, bizarre, and esoteric," Labovitz says. And they are definitely not mainstream. They generally don't have advertising, are not aimed toward a large audience, and usually do not try to make a profit.

Labovitz says e-zines have helped give writers more individual power. "E-zines are a further democratization of publishing and spreading information," he says, adding that, "Today, even without having to print out and photocopy your work, you can make your writings available to many people."

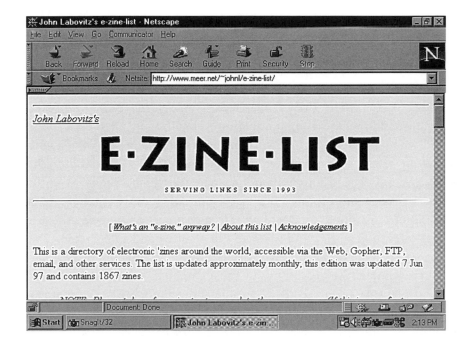

E-zine.list connects you to the world of electronic zines—a vast publishing empire made up of inspired individuals.

As for the future of e-zines, Labovitz feels they will continue to grow. Some e-zines will stop publishing, but there will always be new ones to fill the void.

Café Magazine

When you visit the *Café* magazine Web site (*http://www.gold.net/users/ fy15/david.html*), you might want to have a tall cup of latte nearby. This site was created by people with a passion for the coffee they drink and the cafés where they drink them. The Web magazine originated in England, but has strong production ties with the United States. Bob Biderman, the managing editor, conceived the idea in 1994 along with a group of professional writers and teachers. They ventured onto the Web, mainly because they hadn't seen anything else like it.

The magazine explores the history of cafés, current news about coffees from around the world, the strong connection between the arts and cafés, and stories and poems with a coffee and café theme. This is a popular site for writers who are interested in learning more about where some of the great ideas of the eighteenth and nineteenth century "literally" occurred. In an article about French cafés, the magazine says, "Cafés make the writer a performer. . . . To see yourself writing in the mirrors which abound in Paris cafés, and to know that you are being perceived in the act of writing can be both therapeutic and enjoyable."

What's the future for the Web magazine? According to Mr. Biderman, it's problematic. *Café* lacks the all-important sponsorship, so to make money it has turned to selling a printed version of the magazine as well as pamphlets and books.

Biderman feels that, for now, the Internet is allowing many ideas to circulate and to be exposed to an audience that is much wider and diverse than can be obtained by a printed-press publication. But the writing on the Internet is influenced heavily by multimedia, and he is afraid that people's attention spans are too short for text-based Web sites. He warns Netsurfers that things may change, "Eventually, [the corporate world] will scare people into believing that the Internet is dangerous unless it's contained and money interests are similar to those that now control the rest of the media."

Baudeville

So what did happen to Chiphead Harry? This is the question that thousands of visitors are asked daily when they visit the latest installment of this regular feature at *Baudeville* (*http://www.baudeville.com/baudeville*). *Baudeville* is not the typical e-zine. It has a staff of regular contributors, but also accepts freelance writers.

The e-zine, according to its editor Dan Heath, is a mixture of comedy and commentary. "We seek to entertain our audience through the written word, not to serve as a news source," explains Heath. You will not see any mention of upcoming elections, wars, or sensational Simpson-like trials. Heath wants articles that are ahead of the mainstream news media. He seeks offbeat topics that are opinionated and well researched. "Our favorite topics are those that the *New York Times* will cover six months from now and think they discovered them," says Heath.

Dan Heath has some strong opinions about the future of the Internet and what it will mean for writers, but he makes it clear that they are just *his* opinions. "Don't listen to anyone who claims to have an answer [on where the Internet is going]," he warns. He feels that the Internet will become more centralized. "Just as the novelty of the Xerox paper zine eventually wore off, the number of people who are willing to operate quality sites, for the love it, with no commercial intentions, will diminish quickly," contends Heath.

Heath believes novice Internet users will want a "nice 'n' easy guide" to get around the Internet, and the corporate world will provide it for them. "This does not bode well for magazines like *Baudeville* because it is experimentation that allows us to survive," Heath says. "And this experimentation will drop off as newbie Net users seek paved roads and eschew uncharted ground."

What will this mean for writers on the Internet? Heath says the trend of more graphics and less words isn't good news for writers. "There will be an increasing market for fully developed Web features, including the HTML work and graphics, rather than text articles alone," says Heath. To work effectively on the Internet, writers might need to take on responsibilities that formerly belonged to publishers and designers, such as knowing and implementing HTML or working closely with partners who do.

Urban Desires

Urban Desires (*http://www.desires.com*) on the World Wide Web publishes articles about sex, music, food, art, and travel. "*Urban Desires* is designed with a very broad market in mind," says editor-in-chief Gabrielle Shannon. The magazine, based in New York City, debuted in November 1994 under the banner "Interactive Magazine of Metropolitan Passions." Since then, it has become one of the leading Web magazines.

What is the secret of *Urban Desires*'s success? One might be that she has stuck with its original magazine-model format and just kept improving on it. "Our philosophy at *Desires* is to follow the model we've created, but to expand it as time goes on," states Shannon. *Desires* also got its start when the Web wasn't so full of sound, animation, or graphics. According to Shannon, they didn't have as many opinions back then either. "Back in 1994, the Web looked a lot more like print publishing than it does now," she says. If *Desires* were to start up now, would things look different? "It wouldn't be too far off, because in the end, when you are trying to communicate ideas, you want people to be able to find them."

"Never before has the literary elite so lacked control," says Shannon, adding that, "Unhampered by postage and paper costs, the Internet allows most anyone with the vision, talent, and some technical knowledge to publish what he or she wants." Shannon concedes that there isn't a lot of writing on the Internet making money, yet. But writers are benefiting from increased visibility. She thinks the people who will prosper the most on the Internet are the writers who master this new medium. "We will see a new breed of writers who will become the stars of the new medium," says Shannon. "They will be the ones who will live and breathe the Internet and their mastery will be an organic one."

Salon

Walt Whitman wrote, "I hear America singing, the varied carol I hear." In today's media of talk radio, cable TV, twenty-four-hour news, and the like, is it possible to still hear each American's song? One of the leading Web magazines, *Salon* (*http://www.salon1999.com/*), has set out to "hear all of America singing." And, from all indications, it is doing a pretty good job of listening, so far.

A quick touch of the cursor on "Who are *Salon*," and one has to be impressed with the staff the San Francisco–based magazine has gathered. Many *Salon* staffers are seasoned journalists from leading magazines and newspapers who have come together, according to its mission statement, to "thrash out cultural issues." "We're dedicated to good writing for people who read," says Scott Rosenberg, senior editor. He says the only other sites that are heading in this direction are *Feed* and *Slate*.

But what makes *Salon* different? Rosenberg says it's the interaction with its readers. The *Salon* site includes a conversation forum called Table Talk. "This is where our writers and readers mix it up; it's where we try to make good on the medium's claim to be interactive," says Rosenberg, "We think this kind of exchange—thoughtful, lively, and open—is more truly interactive than flashy multimedia bells and whistles."

Salon aims to foster a lively discussion about cultural affairs through book reviews, writing on art articles, and idea pieces. *Salon*'s aim is to try to create a place on the Web for discussions like those that might have taken place in the mid fifties and sixties in a Greenwich Village bar or at a North Beach bookstore.

Salon is more concerned with the written word than the latest technology. Editors make it clear from the beginning that they are not a "techno-cult," but that they do not look down at Web sites that focus on the latest technology. Rosenberg says, "There's plenty of room on the Web for sites that are obsessed with the latest in technology and those, like ours, that take a more measured view and approach."

Writer's Resource Center

If you were about to buy a house, you wouldn't put down money before giving the house a good look over, right? The same logic applies on the Internet. You need to look around to see the various literary Web sites before trying to get published. "Check out their pages first and try to get an idea of their style and content," says John Hewitt, editor of the Writer's Resource Center (*http://www/azstarnet.com/ ~poewar/writer/writer.html*).

The Writer's Resource Center offers visitors advice on getting published and links to the latest industry news. According to Hewitt, the

Internet has brought a great amount of power to the writer. Anyone who wants to publish can do so at very little cost and with the potential of a worldwide audience. But he reminds writers that such power is not an automatic key to success. "When writers put themselves into the position of the publisher, they inherit the problems and responsibilities that come with it," Hewitt says. "They must learn to promote their work, which can be a delicate task."

Hewitt doesn't see the Internet as the main source of cash flow for any writer. Most literary sites are the result of the hard work of a single person or small group of people. "Rather than [using the] Internet only, writers should use the Internet as part of an overall strategy," Hewitt says. "This is still, for the most part, the same America and same world as before. The key is to serve the [public's] need and desires while publishing something that is important to you."

Writers Net

The old saying goes, "It's not what you know, it's who you know." While many people would beg to differ, connections certainly don't hurt. That's the purpose behind Writers Net (*http://www.writers.net*), a Web site created to facilitate that all-important connection between a writer, an editor, a publisher, or an agent.

Stephen Spencer, editor of Writers Net, says he began the service because he knows how important the connection is between the writer and the people who can get his or her work published. "I can appreciate the difficulties that come with a career in writing—the difficulties of breaking into the field, the difficulties of making money from writing, and the difficulties of making connections," says Spencer.

Writers Net doesn't list just anybody. To be included, you need to have published at least one book in the last seven years, three short stories or poems in the last five years, or three articles in the last eighteen months. You also have to check your e-mail regularly, according to Spencer. Literary agents must explicitly state in their description if they require reading fees.

Spencer explains that there are many benefits from having your named listed on Writers Net. He said writers can get assignments from publishers and editors, find representation from agents, and form friendships and alliances with other like-minded writers.

The Web site is currently run by Spencer alone, but he hopes one day to get corporate sponsorship so the service can expand.

■

Copyright Issues on the Internet— Today and Tomorrow

Adam Steinback

Writers, publishers, journalists, editors, librarians, and others who work with words need to understand copyright laws and how they apply in new digital mediums, particularly the Internet's World Wide Web. All kinds of written expression are legally protected under U.S. and international copyright laws, no matter what the distribution medium, but new technologies have made these legal protections difficult to enforce. This chapter provides an overview in layman's terms of basic copyright concerns of which writers must be aware.

Today

Today, writers are concerned about protecting their creations, and rightfully so. Let's say you just finished writing a great novel and you want to copyright it. Well, don't worry; you've just secured one. In the U.S. and most other countries, a work is copyrighted as soon as it is created. You don't even need help from an attorney. In fact, it's protected whether you've distributed it, just printed it out, or even if it's only on a floppy or hard disk. The owner of a copyright has the exclusive rights to reproduce the work, sell and distribute the work, prepare derivative works, and display the work publicly. No special legal formalities or paperwork are necessary, such as registering the work with the Copyright Office or issuing a copyright notice. In fact, as of March 1, 1989, the requirement that copyright notice be placed on creative works was eliminated from the U.S. copyright law.

Even though you have the copyright as soon as you create a work, there are still valid reasons why one would go to the expense and trouble to register the work with the Copyright Office in Washington, D.C. Registration gives the copyright owner some important extra benefits. First, securing the certificate of registration is legal and tangible proof of the validity of the copyright and the truthfulness of the statements made in the copyright application. This can come in handy if anyone ever challenges your copyright, such as filing a lawsuit and taking it to court. Second, registration must be made before an infringement occurs in order to qualify to receive legal damages, particularly "statutory damages" that a copyright owner may be eligible for if actual damages are hard to prove. Last, registration is necessary to file suit for copyright infringement upon a work. To register, you have to mail in the application form (Form TX for text works), a $20 registration fee, and two copies of the work to: Copyright Office, Washington, D.C. 20559.

A digital version of an authored work is entitled to copyright protection if it meets the basic legal requirements. After satisfying these criteria, it is protected. Even though work in a digital form is not tangible and only exists on a computer "in the ones and zeros of binary code," this does not affect copyright protection. Computer "language" is protected under copyright laws just like works in tangible mediums, such as print or recorded broadcasts. Under copyright law, the moment a work of authorship is created, it is automatically protected by copyright to the extent that it meets three requirements: It must be original, that is, not copied from others; minimally creative; and fixed in a tangible medium of expression.

All three requirements are easily met in the online world. First, the originality requirement poses no special problems; a work is sufficiently original if it was independently created and not copied from other works. The question arises here: how different must a work be from an original source to be copyrightable? The legal answer is that an edited work becomes copyrightable at the point when it is a unique and distinguishable variation from the original work; minimal changes will not suffice. For example, if one is manipulating text supplied by a client, he or she must make sure that the client has obtained appropriate permissions to protect both the writer and the client.

Second, the amount of creativity required is very slight; a work is protected if it's merely the product of the most minimal creativity. Unlike the opening example, it by no means has to be a complete epic novel, nor unique, innovative, or even possess any redeeming quality to pass the creativity test.

Last, a work deemed original and minimally creative must then also be fixed in a tangible medium of expression. This includes works printed or recorded, among other means, but disqualifies words that are simply thought or spoken. Fortunately, there are many ways for digital authors to "fix" an expression in a tangible medium because the Internet falls under this category as it is converted to a digital format. For example, it can be fixed on digital storage media such as a CD-ROM or Zip disk, a bulletin board system or online service, an online database, an e-mail or Usenet message, or even a Web page. These all qualify as tangible and permanent physical media under copyright law.

Despite these relatively simple guidelines, copyright infringement continually occurs in the online world, particularly on the Internet, which isn't centrally controlled or supervised by anybody. Additionally, other technologies, such as fax machines, copiers, and scanners, make copying very easy. Some online users even have the mistaken idea that any work available online can be freely copied, distributed, and otherwise used without permission.

Before distributing their works online, authors must realize that copying digital information is dangerously easy. And once copied, it is easy to redistribute by posting it on the Internet where it can be retrieved by a computer user anywhere in the world. Digital copies can be and are made very cheaply and quickly, and they can last as long as the data is not erased. The origin of digital works can also be easily disguised by making minor changes to the content.

Let's say a writer puts his or her work on the Internet, but wants to allow certain people to reuse it, without infringing upon his or her copyright. Authors can do this by granting a license giving someone permission to use their work. This is a common practice in the online world. For example, the owners of commercial computer databases like Lexis-Nexis only grant access to users who sign license agreements and agree to pay access fees. Such agreements, however, usually don't give the licensee full rights to the content. They may not, for example, be allowed to distribute the material to others.

Still, as a practical matter, granting such licenses does not prevent unauthorized copying. Once a user has paid for a legitimate copy of something, there is no practical way to prevent him or her from making other unauthorized copies. A content provider's best protection is to make obvious his or her license restrictions. To ensure that a license is enforceable, don't bury it under multiple links; instead, make the user look at it before gaining access to the site. Also include a detailed and specific copyright notice, or at least the © symbol with your full name and the year of creation or publication, whichever is first. Here's an example of a quite reasonable online license that one might find at a Web site:

> COPYRIGHT OWNER provides the information on this server to anyone, but retains copyright on all text and graphic images. This means that you may not: distribute the text or graphics to others without the express written permission of COPYRIGHT OWNER, "mirror" or include this information on your own server or documents without our permission, or modify or reuse the text or graphics on this system. You may: print copies of the information for your own personal use; store the files on your own computer for your personal use only, and reference hypertext documents on this server from your own documents.

Another legal principle, *fair use*, loosens copyright restrictions, in this case, for the entire public. Fair use is a use of someone else's work that is generally allowed under copyright law. For example, newsworthy or educational uses are likely to fall under the fair use category. The factors for whether a use is a fair use or an infringement are: (1) the purpose and character of the use, including whether or not it is for profit, (2) the character of the copyrighted work, (3) how much of the total work is used in the course of use, and (4) what effect the use will have on the market for or value of the work being copied.

Another way works can be freely used may be more obvious. Copying an old work, "one no longer protected by copyright," is legal. After all, copyright is for a limited amount of time, so when it expires the work goes into the public domain; it becomes owned by the public and may be freely copied by anyone. Now you're probably wondering how long a copyright lasts. The term of a copyright is the creator's life plus fifty years. For works created anonymously, under a pseudonym, or as a work for hire, the term is either seventy-five years from first publication or a hundred years from its creation, whichever is shorter. For works created by more than one person the term is the life of the last surviving creator plus fifty years.

Tomorrow

Enforcement of copyright laws in the digital age has become a major problem for writers. Something clearly needs to be done to fix the current dilemma of how easy it is to copy protected works. Digital documents, unlike written ones, can very easily be manipulated, reproduced, and distributed. Various technology-based solutions have been proposed to address the problem of copyright infringement, such as micropayments and encryption technology. Encryption algorithm schemes translate digital works into unreadable gibberish, similar to what the military does with top-secret messages. One idea that combines these two techniques proposes to use the Federal Reserve as a depository of electronic keys. A consumer would transfer a micropayment from his or her account to the copyright owner's account to purchase an electronic decryption key that would unlock the information purchased.

Using the Federal Reserve for this function may be sensible in a society such as ours that is based on an information economy, where information is money. Just as the government currently supervises banks, in the future it could regulate the distribution of rights to digital information. Research is also under way on another system called digital signatures. These are used to electronically embed a digital signature into a work, which enables the copyright owner to track and identify his or her product even if it's been heavily altered or modified. A variation of this technique is used today to trace expensive artwork in case of theft. Some experts speculate that such effective electronic means could eventually leave current copyright laws impotent. Others more radically predict that when these technologies are widely introduced, copyright may altogether lose its importance as a way for content providers to protect their works.

After all, the simple fact is that copyright laws have never effectively prevented private individuals from making unauthorized copies. What they have done, and likely will continue to do, even in the online era, is deter the big players, the megamedia corporations from stealing others' works. For example, because they're afraid of being sued for infringement, publishers are seeking permission from their authors to reproduce the authors' preexisting works online, and are also making sure that publishing agreements for new works address electronic rights. For the same reason, commercial online services like America Online and Internet service providers try to prevent copyrighted material from being placed on their systems without permission and quickly remove it when they find it.

For a detailed discussion of copyright and other legal issues faced by writers on- and offline, see Tad Crawford and Tony Lyon's book, *The Writer's Legal Guide* (Allworth Press).

■

Learning to Make
Your Writing Electric

Chip Rowe

If you've ever spent any time online, you've stumbled across a World Wide Web home page that highlights its creator's writing, design work, or general obsessions. The Internet can make anyone into a Citizen Hearst. From *Aisle Say* ("The Internet Magazine of Stage Reviews"), to *DaveNet* ("Amusing Rants from Dave Winer's Desktop"), to *Desire Street* ("The Electronic Chapbook of the New Orleans Poetry Forum"), to *Nadine* ("The Magazine That Wishes It Were a Band"), and *Word Heaven* ("Satire, Poems, and an Ad for My Screenplays"), thousands of self-made publishers have staked out their plots in digital space.

One of the benefits of online publishing is that it all but eliminates the printing and distribution costs involved in publishing your work; another is that it puts your writing in a stream of words where it can be discovered and appreciated—maybe even with cash. By launching an electronic magazine, a writer can make his or her articles, essays, poetry, observations, and other wisdom, accessible to tens of millions of readers (and, perhaps eventually, all of humanity).

There are thousands of e-zines available on the World Wide Web and by e-mail. Each day, more writers like Herbert Gambill add to the list. "I can hardly speak with authority," he told me. "But perhaps I can encourage others by explaining how a numskull like me could learn how to do an online zine in a few days and then have the first issue up within a month. Like many writers, I always wanted to publish a magazine but never had the money. On the Internet, I can publish a color edition with sound clips at no more cost than the $30 I already pay each month for online access."

The Easy E-zine Format

I won't go into the logistics of getting wired beyond suggesting that beginners sign on with a service like America Online for a point-and-click introduction. Once you've become familiar with the larger Internet and what other writers have done online, you'll be ready to contemplate your own electric presence. After several years of publishing in various digital formats, I've concluded that online publishing is a lot like everything else. At first, your mind races through the possibilities, but as you become more experienced, you return to simpler pleasures.

There are many ways to present your e-zine, especially on the World Wide Web. But the equivalent of the "simpler pleasures" is known as ASCII (pronounced *as-kee*). It is nothing more than your words deposited on the page—no **bold**, *italic*, <u>underline</u>, graphics, or varying type sizes. ASCII text can be read by any computer in existence. That may not be the sexiest way to produce a publication, but it is the simplest and most widely accepted.

Some writers create an ASCII version and leave it at that. Others prefer more complicated, graphically intensive formats. Still, others have the patience to produce each issue in several formats, including a print version. Whatever format you choose, you'll spend many more hours perfecting the online version, since it's never committed to paper and you can fiddle with it until the end of time.

Many writers believe ASCII makes for better online publications. Without graphics and photos, the words become that much more important. Alex Swain of the e-zine *Whatever Ramblings* notes, "Because of their lack of material presence, plain-text zines need an extra boost in the literary department. Being descriptive is the only way around not having pictures or drawings. After you write something, go back and pretend that you're an innocent reader of the text. Can you see it? Is it concise? Does it flow?"

In his online newsletter, the *Network Observer*, Phil Agre emphasizes the importance of saying something new. "Most everything on the Net consists of people saying things they've heard elsewhere," he writes. "People really appreciate it if you say something original." The currency of the Net is information, and the fresh, compelling information stands out.

Tips for Formatting

Creating an ASCII zine is not a complicated process, but following a few guidelines will make publishing even easier. Any word processing software, including SimpleText, DOS Editor, Microsoft Word, and WordPerfect, can create ASCII text. Simply use the "Save As" function on your document and save your file as "plain text" or "text with line breaks." Here are some formatting suggestions:

- Remember that your work is going to appear on a computer screen. Keep your paragraphs short and to the point. Don't let your line lengths exceed fifty to fifty-five characters. If you do, your readers may get odd line breaks that make your writing look like barbed wire.
- Rather than indenting paragraphs, put a blank line between them. Don't use tabs.
- Don't split words with hyphens (it makes your e-zine more difficult to read and search).
- Place a "hard" return at the end of every line of text. You do this by hitting the "Enter" or "Return" key. It's a necessary hassle.
- Avoid special characters such as curly quotes. Saving your file as plain text should resolve this, but be alert.
- At the top of your publication, include its title, number, date, and a tagline explaining its mission or purpose. Also include a table of contents and an e-mail address where readers can reach you.
- Keep the size of each issue to a minimum, especially if you plan to distribute your e-zine by e-mail. Any issue that weighs in at more than 60K is probably too much. The last issue of my e-zine was 6,200 words and totaled 38K, and I found that manageable. Remember, the more easily digested your e-zine is, the more voracious readers you'll have.
- Include a copyright notice (or anticopyright notice, if you pre-

fer) and specify under what circumstances your writing may be redistributed.

Even if you later decide to publish your e-zine in other formats, I recommend always making an ASCII version. That way you aren't limiting your audience. You can still have fun creating a version that rubs its belly, blows bubbles, and walks backward at the same time.

Helpful Software

There are two methods for distributing your e-zine so that it can include color, photos, icons, graphics, and even sound. The first is the World Wide Web. The second is to use an authoring program such as Adobe Acrobat, which retails for about $300. The software that readers need to view an e-zine created with Acrobat is free, widely distributed, and runs on just about any computer. You'll often see Acrobat files described as PDF files.

Herbert Gambill, who publishes a in PDF, has this to say about the format: "When assembling a publication with Acrobat, you can create links from words within each document, thumbnails of all the pages for quick reference, and clickable notes. I used those in one of my screenplays to explain screenplay formatting. That way, those readers familiar with screenplays can just skip over the notes."

"Creating Acrobat documents is easy," he adds. "You just prepare your document in a word processor or drawing program. But instead of printing it on paper, you send it to the software, which prepares it as a PDF file. You are then able to insert pages, replace pages, add links, add notes, create bookmarks, and so forth, until you are ready to save it as the final document for distribution."

Acrobat does have some disadvantages. Unless a reader has already downloaded the viewer software, he or she may hesitate at the extra time and disk space required. Because of the graphics, your Acrobat-created e-zine may be a huge file in itself, which can also discourage readers. I've never used Acrobat to publish my e-zine, mainly because of the expense, but many people swear by it. I chose instead to create format-specific applications. That is, I did an abbreviated ASCII version, then a Mac version that included photos, sounds, and other gizmos, then a DOS version.

For the Mac version I used a shareware program called DocMaker, which costs $25. It has many features similar to Acrobat, but not the cross-platform flexibility. For my DOS version, I used shareware called Writer's Dream, which costs $30. Writer's Dream is not nearly as versatile as DocMaker (for instance, you can't change font sizes), but it does the trick. Like many other inexpensive DOS authoring programs, it is basically an enhanced ASCII reader that allows for color backgrounds and word searches.

There are many other digital authoring programs available, but I found that most were not intuitive enough to allow the average nontechnical user to navigate through them. Many of my readers were puzzled even trying to master Writer's Dream, which I thought had a no-brainer interface.

All that said, I had a blast creating my e-zine and sharing my work. An authoring program allows you to create a digital publication just as you would on paper, complete with cover and photographs and color, at little or no cost. It adds an interactive dimension as well by allowing you to link elements through icons and include sound files, such as a greeting I recorded welcoming people to the issue.

No matter what format you chose, you should test your e-zine thoroughly before distributing it. In the case of an ASCII zine, e-mail a draft to a few friends before posting it more widely. With more complicated e-zines, test your work on as many machines and with as many readers as you can. You don't want "buggy" copies of your writing floating around the Net, because you'll never catch up with them.

Webbing in Readers

Because the Internet is so expansive, and because most people will stumble across your writing rather than seek it out, it's a good idea to distribute your work to as many places as possible. You can contribute your publication to libraries such as those maintained by the Writers' Club on America Online or to any of the numerous archives on the Internet. With ASCII zines, e-mail is an option. Build a subscriber list of regular readers and anyone else who requests your e-zine (it's not good netiquette to mail your work unsolicited, and for privacy's sake, send out copies individually or use the blind carbon-copy function available on most e-mail programs).

Once you've mastered the ASCII format, consider creating your own World Wide Web site. Many excellent books have been written on how to create Web pages, and free tutorials are available online.

In the simplest terms, the Web is a series of online files that can be read by software known as browsers. Popular browsers include Netscape Navigator and Microsoft Internet Explorer. When readers type in your Web address, they are taken to a page not unlike what they'd see in a paper magazine. It might include color graphics, photos, text of various sizes and links—in the form of highlighted words, graphics, or photos—that, when clicked, take them to another spot on the Web or another page at your site.

Web documents are created in hypertext markup language. The HTML coding is added to ASCII files to tell the browsers how to display them. To make a word **bold**, for example, you add < b > before the word and < /b > after. There are many programs available to help you convert existing text documents into HTML, and in chapter 16 you will find an introduction to HTML.

Herbert Gambill describes his experiences with putting his zine on the Web this way: "Legend has it that when Buster Keaton first started performing in films, he took a camera apart to see how it works. That's also how most people first learn HTML: they download the source code of a favorite page. There is little to learn, just a few formatting tags, how to add images to your document, creating hypertext links, and so forth. HTML sounds complicated, but you'll be astounded how simple it is."

If you'd like to learn more about publishing your writing online, I've created a World Wide Web page to help (point your browser to *http://thetransom.com/chip/zines*). The page includes links to the e-zines, software, and tutorials mentioned in this chapter. A. J. Liebling once said that, "Freedom of the press belongs to those who own one." Connected to the Net, you do.

Chip Rowe compiled and edited The Zine Reader, *an anthology*
*of great zine writing published by Henry Holt (*www.zinebook.com*).*

■

Web Publishing: A Guide to Essential HTML

Thomas J. Timmons

For the writer looking to publish or advertise on the Internet, even the terminology associated with Web publishing is daunting. While the names are confusing, many of the basic concepts are rather simple. Hypertext markup language (HTML) is merely a text document with formatting codes (or tags) to tell the viewing software—browsers—how to organize and display the document.

Simple? Yes. Complex? Yes, it is that as well. Made up of numerous simple elements, HTML is the foundation upon which the World Wide Web is built. Simple enough for just about anyone to learn, it is robust enough to support animated graphics, fill-in forms, background music, and much, much more. Anyone with the ability to create text documents and upload files to an Internet server can create Web pages.

In 1994, explaining HTML publishing would have been relatively simple. The informal documentation of HTML had been clarified and formalized, and a "Request for Comments" had been published on the Internet to allow all Web authors to begin harmonizing their use of the language. It would never be that simple again. What happened? In a word, Netscape.

The consensus-based design of HTML would be forever changed by the use of Netscape *extensions*—HTML commands that only the

Netscape Navigator Web browser understood. Rather than wait for the Internet Engineering Task Force to create new HTML specifications for advanced features, Netscape Communications Corporation started releasing its new browsers with the ability to use new features, counting on Web masters to start using the new commands before any official specification was released. Browser-specific HTML commands are possible because Web browsers are designed to ignore any command that they do not understand. For example, a tag may be used to change the color of a given area of text. A browser that does not have the capability to display the new tag will keep the text black. In 1995, the entry of Microsoft into the Web browser market with Internet Explorer added yet a new layer of complexity to the equation. Microsoft's browser, which was in its 3.0 release as this was written, supported commands that even Netscape didn't use.

The current specification for HTML is called 3.2 and was released as a working draft on September 9, 1996. However, the competition between Netscape and Microsoft to dominate the browser market means that with each new release of each company's respective products, support for new features is continually growing. By the time you read this, both companies will have released new products with new capabilities and will be giving them away in an attempt to tighten their control on the market.

So what is a prospective Web author to do? My advice: keep it simple. For the vast majority of those wishing to begin publishing on the Web, knowledge of just a few HTML commands and a small number of Netscape and Internet Explorer extensions are all that is necessary to get started. As your proficiency increases, more commands can be added to your pages. Remember, each new HTML standard is designed to be backwardly compatible with previous versions, so your page will still function, even as HTML continually changes.

What sort of commands are required for a beginner?
- Standard HTML tags required for Web page creation (these let Web browsers know your document is an HTML document)
- Tags to place graphics on your pages
- Tags to format text, and to determine the color of text and page backgrounds
- Tags to create links to other files on the Internet

What sort of commands won't be discussed here?

- Tables
- Frames
- Animated graphics
- Fill-in forms
- Java and other plug-in programs

For more information on these features, consult the list of references at the end of the chapter.

Writing Web Documents

Web documents, from the simplest text-only pages to the wildest multimedia experiences, are all based on the same basic HTML structure: a simple text document marked up with formatting codes or tags. Although the complexity of HTML has skyrocketed since 1994, it is still possible to use a simple text editor to create interesting, professional-looking pages for the Web.

Anyone planning on using forms, tables, Java applets, or other interactive features is advised to use an HTML writing package. These programs automate much of the HTML coding that would otherwise drive a would-be Web writer mad.

How HTML Tags Are Structured

Tags are set off from regular text by the use of the less-than and greater-than signs, < and >. Since these data characters are used as part of the document-formatting language, it is recommended that if you have a need in your text for one of these symbols, to use an *entity reference* or a *character reference*. This eliminates the possibility that browser software will try to read your text as a tag. (The references for greater-than are &gt or &#62 and for less-than are &lt or &#60. Since the ampersand is also used in references, it is sometimes advisable to use &amp or &#38 to display an ampersand.) For more information on entity references, consult the list of HTML-coded characters later in this chapter.

Presented below are the essential HTML tags that every Web designer should know. There are many more tags included in the specification of HTML 3.2, but the following will allow the novice Web designer to begin to stake out territory on the new electronic frontier.

Types of Tags

Most HTML tags currently in use can be broken down into four simple categories:

- Tags used to tell the browser that the file it is reading is an HTML document
- Tags used to format text (including lists and tables)
- Tags used to link the file with other files, actions, or other locations within the current file
- Tags used to place images into the document

Format of Tags

While much on the Internet is "case sensitive" (e.g., the file TEST.TXT is not the same as Test.Txt) due to the Unix operating system upon which much of the Internet is built, HTML itself is "case insensitive." That is, the tag < TITLE > < /TITLE > is exactly the same as < title > < /title > and the same as < TitLe > < /tItLE > . It is usually recommended, however, to place tags in ALL CAPS, to make it easier to work on your pages. HTML also ignores extra spaces and hard returns, making it useful to add extra hard returns to your document to separate the various sections of your page for easier editing. When extra returns are not added, it often becomes very difficult to determine where you are in your document. This is especially true with documents that have numerous links, text-formatting codes, images, or tables.

When a tag calls for the use of quotation marks it is very important that *both* the opening and the closing quotes are used. Some browsers will return an error message, or otherwise garble the page if the closing quote mark is omitted.

Tags are usually structured like this: < START-TAG NAME > Text to be "tagged" < /END-TAG NAME >

For example, to put text in bold, you would use the bold tag: < B > This text is bold < /B >

Some tags do not currently have end-tags, such as LINE BREAK, HORIZONTAL RULE, or LIST ITEM. Others, like PARAGRAPH, do

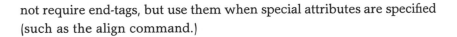

not require end-tags, but use them when special attributes are specified (such as the align command.)

Tags That Must Be Used

HTML documents are made up of two areas: a head and a body. The header area is used to describe the document's title, usage, and relationship with other documents (for advanced Web authors), while the body is the area of main text and images that the person visiting your page will see and interact with. Thus, all HTML documents should have the following four commands: HTML, HEAD, TITLE, AND BODY. Many browsers will allow you to omit either the BODY or the HEAD command, and HTML 3.2 doesn't require them, but it is recommended that you continue to use all four of the "must use" commands for the foreseeable future.

■ **HTML Tag.** Identifies the document as an HTML document.
What to Write: <HTML> begins the document, </HTML> ends it.
Special Instructions: Within the HTML document, there must be a HEAD area and a BODY area. The HTML tag will be the first and last elements of any HTML document.

■ **HEAD Tag.** Provides the browser with information about the document.
What to Write: <HEAD> begins the header area, </HEAD> ends it.
Special Instructions: Within the HEAD tag, there must be a TITLE tag.

■ **TITLE Tag.** Identifies the contents of the document. The title is usually displayed by the browser software in a title list or as a label for the window displaying the document.
What to Write: <TITLE> begins the title line, </TITLE> ends it.
Special Instructions: Titles should be less than sixty-four characters long.

■ **BODY Tag.** Identifies the main text area of the document. It is also used to determine the color of text elements and page background.
What to Write: <BODY> begins the body area, </BODY> ends it.

Special Instructions: Newer browsers will accept special arguments within the BODY tag, which allow either a repeating graphic (a GIF or a JPEG image) to be used as a background pattern, or a specific color to be selected for the background color, text color, and color of hypertext links. The same < /BODY > end-tag is used.

Special Arguments:

- *Background Image:* < BODY BACKGROUND = "filename.gif" > .
- *Specified Background Color:* < BODY BGCOLOR = "#FFFFFF" > where FFFFFF is the hexadecimal description of the color. (See list at end of chapter for the codes for a variety of colors.)
- *Named Background Color:* < BODY BGCOLOR = "WHITE" > where WHITE is one of the accepted common color names. (See list at end of chapter for accepted colors.) Names will also work on the three commands listed below.
- *Specified Text Color:* < BODY TEXT = "#FFFFFF" > .
- *Highlight Color of a Hyperlink:* < BODY LINK = "#FFFFFF" > .
- *Highlight Color of a Previously Used Hyperlink:* < BODY VLINK = "#FFFFFF" > .
- *Highlight Color of a Hyperlink When it is Clicked:* < BODY ALINK = "#FFFFFF" > .

All of the color arguments can be included at the same time (in any order) within a single BODY tag. For example: < BODY BGCOLOR = "#FFFFFF" TEXT = "#000000" LINK = "#FF1493" VLINK = "#00BFFF" ALINK = "#FFFF00" > < /BODY > .

Example HTML Page

< HTML >
< HEAD >
< TITLE > This is an HTML Document < /TITLE > .
< /HEAD >
< BODY BGCOLOR = "#FFFFFF" >
This is the main text of this document.
< /BODY >
< /HTML >
This page will have black text on a white background.

Text-Formatting Tags

■ **COMMENT Tag.** While not technically a text tag, the comment tag is useful as a way to set various sections of the HTML page apart to ease your editing of the document.

What to Write: < ! — begins the comment line, — > ends it.

Special Instructions: Keep comment tags to a single line. If a longer comment is required, use two or more separate comment lines.

■ **PARAGRAPH Tag.** Sets apart text that is to be displayed as a single paragraph of standard text.

What to Write: < P > begins the paragraph, < /P > ends it.

Special Instructions: Currently, there is no requirement for a closing tag in the paragraph tag. However, to use the ALIGN attribute, a closing tag is necessary. The ALIGN command is only supported in newer browsers. To change a paragraph's typeface, use the FONT command (see below).

Special Arguments:

- *Alignment of Paragraphs:* The paragraph command automatically left-justifies text. The ALIGN command allows paragraphs to be centered or right-justified. *A centered paragraph:* < P ALIGN = CENTER > ... < /P >. *A right-justified paragraph:* < P ALIGN = RIGHT > ... < /P >.

■ **HEADING Tag.** Used for headlines, titles, or other short statements that are to be set apart from regular text.

What to Write: < H1 > begins the heading area, < /H1 > ends it.

Special Instructions: The heading tag accepts heading levels from 1 to 6, with decreasing emphasis.

Special Arguments:

- *Alignment of Headings:* Headings, like paragraphs, are usually left-justified. To center or right-justify a heading, use the ALIGN command. *A centered heading:* < H1 ALIGN = CENTER > ... < /H1 >. *A right-justified heading:* < H2 ALIGN = RIGHT > ... < /H2 >.

■ **CENTER Tag.** This Netscape-specific tag allows a block of text, headline, table, or graphic to be centered within the screen of the viewer's browser. Its functionality has been included in the ALIGN command, but support for the center tag is included in HTML 3.2, due to its widespread use. Internet Explorer also supports this tag.

What to Write: < CENTER > begins the centered area, < /CENTER > ends it.

Special Instructions: Be careful, if the closing-tag is omitted, the entire document will be centered.

■ **FONT Tag.** This tag allows text in either headings or paragraphs to be altered in size, color, and typeface. It began as a Netscape-specific tag, but is included in the current draft of HTML 3.2.

What to Write: < FONT > begins the area of text to be modified, < /FONT > ends it.

Special Instructions: The FONT tag can be used in either PARAGRAPH or HEADING text.

Special Arguments:

- *Size:* This modifies the size of the selected text. Values of 1 to 7 are accepted. Both absolute or relative values are accepted. Text has a default value of 3. *To set text to an absolute value of 2:* < FONT SIZE = 2 > ... < /FONT >. *To reduce the font by a (relative) value of 2:* < FONT SIZE = -2 > ... < /FONT >.

- *Color:* This modifies the color of the selected text. Like the BODY BGCOLOR command, either hexadecimal color codes or colors from the list of commonly used color names are allowed. *To set the color of text to red with hexadecimal coding:* < FONT COLOR = "#FF0000" > ... < /FONT >. *To set the color of text to red with a color name:* < FONT COLOR = "red" >. See the list of colors at the end of the chapter for more information.

- *Typeface:* A recent addition to both Internet Explorer and Netscape, the FACE argument instructs the browser to display a specified typeface. It allows a list of names to be specified, in order of preference, in case the person viewing your page doesn't have a particular typeface. Be sure to spell the typeface the same way your computer recognizes it. For example, on my computer, the font Copperplate Bold is known as Copperplate Gothic Bold. Thus, it is important that I put in the full name of the font in the FACE command, or the typeface won't be changed. *To set text to a generic sans-serif font:* < FONT FACE = "Arial, Helvetica, Geneva" > ... < /FONT >.

120

■ **BOLD Tag**. Creates boldface text.

What to Write: <B> begins the bold area, </B> ends it.

Special Instructions: Another tag that serves much the same function is <STRONG> ... </STRONG>.

■ **ITALICS Tag.** Creates italics.

What to Write: <I> begins the italics area, </I> ends it.

Special Instructions: Bold and italics tags can be "nested" within each other to create bold italics. Other tags that serve much the same function as the italics tag are: <ADDRESS> ... </ADDRESS>, <EM> ... </EM>, and <CITE> ... </CITE>.

■ **BLOCKQUOTE Tag**. Creates an indented area of text.

What to Write: <BLOCKQUOTE> begins the indented area, </BLOCKQUOTE> ends it.

Special Instructions: This command indents the selected text from both margins, in the way a quoted passage from a book is usually presented.

■ **PRE Tag.** Formats text as monospaced, Courier typeface.

What to Write: <PRE> begins the area of preformatted text, </PRE> ends it.

Special Instructions: Useful for indicating that the are of text is typewritten or printed from a computer. Also maintains line breaks and spaces, making it possible to line up two or more columns of text without using tables. The TYPEWRITER TEXT tag <TT> ... </TT> also uses Courier, but does not read extra spaces and hard returns. Other tags that serve much the same function as the TYPEWRITER TEXT tag are <CODE> ... </CODE>, <KBD> ... </KBD>, and <SAMP> ... </SAMP>. Note that Internet Explorer displays the KEYBOARD text as bold Courier, as opposed to plain text.

■ **HORIZONTAL Rule Tag.** Creates a screenwide ruling line.

What to Write: <HR> creates a horizontal rule.

Special Instructions: There is no closing tag for a horizontal rule.

Special Arguments: Newer browsers accept the following modifications to the HORIZONTAL RULE tag.

- *Size:* < HR SIZE = "x" >, where x equals the number of pixels high the line will be.
- *Width*: < HR WIDTH = "x%" >, where x equals the percentage of the screen width the line will extend, or < HR WIDTH = "x" >, where x equals the number of pixels wide the line will be.
- *Alignment:* < HR ALIGN = LEFT >; the ALIGN must be used in conjunction with the WIDTH command, or else the alignment will not be noticeable. The ALIGN command also accepts CENTER and RIGHT arguments. All of these arguments can be used within a single HR tag. The default alignment is CENTER.
- *No Shading:* < HR NOSHADE >; the HR command usually creates the impression of an indented line on the screen, with two bands of light shading at the top and bottom of the rule. The NOSHADE argument creates a line of solid color.

■ **LINE BREAK Tag**. Forces an end to the current line of text.
What to Write: < BR > ends the current line of text.
Special Instructions: There is no ending tag for a line break.

■ **ORDERED LIST Tag.** Creates a hierarchically ordered list. Useful when the first item is the most important.
What to Write: < OL > begins the ordered list area, < /OL > ends it.
Special Instructions: Individual items have the LIST ITEM tag.
Example:

> < P >To make a Hot Fudge Sundae, you need: < /P >
> < OL >
> < LI >Vanilla Ice Cream
> < LI >Hot Fudge
> < LI >Whipped Cream
> < LI >A Cherry
> < /OL >

This would result in the following text appearing on the screen:
To make a Hot Fudge Sundae, you need:

1. Vanilla Ice Cream
2. Hot Fudge
3. Whipped Cream
4. A Cherry

■ **UNORDERED LIST Tag**. Creates a bulleted list of items, without any hierarchical order.

What to Write: < UL > begins the ordered list, < /UL > ends it.

Special Instructions: Individual items have LIST ITEM tag.

Special Arguments: Netscape currently allows you to define the style of the bullet used in a list. Look for this capability in Internet Explorer soon.

- *Round Bullet:* < UL TYPE = DISC > ... < /UL >
- *Square Bullet:* < UL TYPE = SQUARE > ... < /UL >
- *Hollow Bullet:* < UL TYPE = CIRCLE > ... < /UL > (Note that even thought this argument is called "CIRCLE", Netscape 3.0 displays it as a hollow square.)

Example:

> < P > To make a Hot Fudge Sundae, you need:
> < UL >
> < LI > Vanilla Ice Cream
> < LI > Hot Fudge
> < LI > Whipped Cream
> < LI > A Cherry
> < /UL >

This would result in the following text appearing on the screen:

> To make a Hot Fudge Sundae, you need:
> - Vanilla Ice Cream
> - Hot Fudge
> - Whipped Cream
> - A Cherry

■ **LIST ITEM Tag.** Lists individual items in an ordered or unordered list.

What to Write: < LI > begins the list item.

Special Instructions: Individual list items do not currently require a closing-tag.

Special Arguments: The TYPE commands in the above example can be used to change individual bullets in the same unordered list.

- *Round Bullet:* < LI TYPE = DISC >
- *Square Bullet:* < LI TYPE = SQUARE >
- *Hollow Bullet:* < LI TYPE = CIRCLE >

Example HTML Page with Text-Formatting Features:
< HTML >
< HEAD >
< TITLE > This is an HTML Document with Text-Formatting < /TITLE >
< /HEAD >
< BODY BGCOLOR = "WHITE" TEXT = "2F4F4F" LINK = "DARKRED"
VLINK = "FF1493" ALINK = "00BFFF" >
< !—This is a Comment line.— >
< H1 > Usually your first line is a heading. < /H1 >
< !—This is the main text area.— >
< P > This is the main text of this document.
< !—Extra hard returns do not show up when the page is viewed.— >
< P ALIGN = RIGHT > This text < B > is in bold < /B >, while this text
< i > is in italics < /i > . This text < B > < I > is in bold italics < /i > < /B > .
Nested format tags should always follow the formula First In, Last Out.
If the text is bolded first, then italicized, the italics should have its closing tag before the bold closing tag. < /P >
< PRE > This text is in monospaced Courier typeface. < /PRE >
< !—This is a list area.— >
< P > This is an unordered list: < /P >
< UL >
< LI TYPE = DISC > Item One
< LI TYPE = SQUARE > Item Two
< LI TYPE = CIRCLE > And So On...
< /UL >
< HR > < P > It is not necessary to put each tag on its own line, but it
is simpler to modify a file that has each tag on its own line, with many
hard returns setting apart various sections. < BR >

HORIZONTAL RULES and LINE BREAKS are good at setting apart
areas of text:
< BR >
< HR ALIGN = CENTER SIZE = 5 WIDTH = 50% >
< H2 > Sometimes you need subheads in your document. < /H2 >
< P > This text is < FONT SIZE = + 7 > really big! < /FONT > < /P >
< P > This text is < FONT COLOR = YELLOW > yellow. < /FONT > < /P >
< P > Be careful with your use of color. Sometimes it is hard for people
to read your page if your colors are not chosen carefully. < /P >

<CENTER> <P>It is often a good idea to put the date the file was last updated at the end of your document so people will know that they have hit the end of the page, as well as giving them an idea of how current your site is. </P> </CENTER>
<I>Today's Date</I>
</BODY>
</HTML>

Linking Tags

The linking or "anchor" tag <A> ... </A> is often considered to be a single tag with two specific purposes; first, to link to another file or place in a document, and, second, to set an anchor point for future linking. However, since the terms *link* and *anchor* describe two completely different actions, I am treating them as two tags.

■ **ANCHOR Tag.** The anchor tag allows the linking tag A HREF (see below) to be used to jump to a specific part of a remote document, or to navigate within the current document.

What to Write: <A NAME = "EXAMPLE"> begins the anchor area, </A> ends it.

Special Instructions: Once an anchor has been set, the A HREF command may be used to direct the browser to that anchor. The text within the anchor area will *not* be highlighted.

■ **LINKING Tag.** Allows the current document to link to another file or to a specific place in a file. This is the feature around which the entire Web was constructed.

What to Write: <A HREF = "file.NAME"> begins the hyperlink area, </A> ends it.

Special Instructions: The text within the <A HREF>...</A> command will be highlighted with a special color (usually blue) to indicate that clicking on this text will take you to a different Web document. Since this command interacts with the rest of the Internet, the file name reference is case sensitive.

Special Arguments: There are a number of ways of using the linking tag.

• *Navigating Within a Document:* <A HREF = "#EXAMPLE">text

</A>; clicking on the highlighted word *text* will take you to the place in the current document that has the anchor name EXAMPLE.

- *Linking to a Local Document:* <A HREF = "file.NAME"> text </A>; clicking on the highlighted word *text* will take you to the document named file.NAME, which is in the same directory as the current document.

- *Linking to a Specific Place in Local Document:* <A HREF = "file. name#EXAMPLE" > text </A>; clicking on the highlighted word *text* will take you to the anchor <A NAME = "EXAMPLE" > in the document named file.NAME, which is in the same directory as the current document.

- *Linking to a Remote Document:* <A HREF = "http://www.test.com/ file.NAME" >text </A>; clicking on the highlighted word *text* will take you to the document named file.NAME, which is located at the Web address www.test.com.

- *Linking to a Specific Place in a Remote Document:* <A HREF = "http://www.test.com/file. NAME#EXAMPLE" >text </A>; clicking on the highlighted word *text* will take you to the anchor EXAMPLE in the document named file.NAME, which is located on a remote server at the Web address www.test.com.

- *Using File Transfer Protocol:* <A HREF = "ftp://ftp.test.com/ " >text </A>; clicking on the highlighted word *text* will take you to the file transfer protocol (FTP) server of the Internet domain test.com.

- *Using Gopher:* <A HREF = "gopher://test.com/" >text </A>; clicking on the highlighted word *text* will take you to the Gopher site of the Internet domain test.com.

- *Sending Mail:* <A HREF = "mailto:sample@test.com" >text </A>; clicking on the highlighted word *text* will send e-mail to the Internet address sample@test.com.

- *Reading Newsgroups:* <A HREF = "news:name.of.group" >text </A>; clicking on the highlighted word *text* will access the Newsgroup name.of.group. (This feature is not supported on all browsers.)

- *Using an Image as a Hyperlink:* <A HREF = "file.NAME" > <IMG SRC = "example.gif" > </A>; clicking on the highlighted image example.gif will take you to the document file.NAME. To indicate that it is a hyperlinked image, it will have a blue border surrounding it.

Sample HTML Page with Links:

< HTML >

< HEAD >

< TITLE > This Is an HTML Document with Links. < /TITLE >

< /HEAD >

< BODY >

< !—Here is the Table of Contents— >

< P > The following are some uses of the A HREF tag:

< P >

< A HREF = "#LINK" > Linking to Another File < /A > < BR >

< A HREF = "#LINK_TO_REMOTE" > Linking to a Remote File < /A > < BR >

< A HREF = "#FTP" > Using an FTP Link < /A > < BR >

< A HREF = "#MAIL" > Using a Mail Link < /A > < BR >

< A HREF = "#GOPHER" > Using a Gopher Link < /A > < BR >

< A HREF = "#NEWS" > Using a Usenet Link < /A > < BR >

< P > Click on any of the above to move to the section desired. < /P >

< !—Here are the Subject Areas.— >

< HR >

< A NAME = "LINK" > Linking to another file < /A > < BR >

< A HREF = "anotherfile.html" > Clicking here < /A > will take you to the file anotherfile.html.

< HR >

< A NAME = "LINK_TO_REMOTE" > Linking to a Remote File < /A > < BR >

< A HREF = "http://www.anothersite.com/anotherfile.html" > Clicking here < /A > will take you to the file anotherfile.html, located on the Web server of anothersite.com.

< HR >

< A NAME = "FTP" > Linking to an FTP Server < /A > < BR >

< A HREF = "ftp://ftp.anothersite.com/anotherfile.exe" > Clicking here < /A > will retrieve the file anotherfile.exe using the FTP server of anothersite.com.

< HR >

< A NAME = "MAIL" > Using an e-mail Link < /A > < BR >

< A HREF = "mailto:myname@mysite.com" > Clicking here < /A > will

send mail from your browser to the e-mail address myname@
mysite.com.

< HR >
< A NAME = "GOPHER" > Linking to a Gopher Server < /A > < BR >
< A HREF = "gopher://gopher.anothersite.com" > Clicking here < /A >
will allow you to browse the gopher server on anothersite.com.

< HR >
< A NAME = "NEWS" > Linking to a Usenet Newsgroup < /A > < BR >
< A HREF = "news:name.of.group" > Clicking here < /A > will allow you
to browse the Usenet Newsgroup name.of.group.

< /BODY >
< /HTML >

Image Placement Tags

■ **IN-LINE IMAGE Tag.** Places an image in your page.

What to Write: < IMG SRC = "example.gif" > places a graphic on
your screen.

Special Instructions: While the GIF format has long been the most
common image format on the Web, now nearly all browsers will accept either GIF or JPEG in-line images. Using the full Web address of
a remote image can allow you to place an image stored on a remote
Web server on your page. < IMG SRC = "http://www.sitename.com/
example.gif" > will place the image example.gif from the Web site
www.sitename.com. Be sure to get permission before using other
people's images.

Special Arguments: Additional arguments may be added between the
IMG and the SRC in any order or combination. They include:

- *Alternative Representation:* The ALT command displays text on
  browsers that cannot display in-line images, or on certain browsers prior to the download of the image. < IMG ALT = "Text"
  SRC = "example.gif" >; the word *Text* will be displayed in the place
  where the image example.gif would normally be shown.
- *Alignment:* The basic ALIGN commands, TOP, MIDDLE, and
  BOTTOM determine how the image aligns itself with the text its
  is adjacent to. < IMG ALIGN = TOP SRC = "example.gif" > would
  align the top of the image example.gif with the top of the line of
  text. If the text wraps on the right-hand side of the page, it will

skip down to the bottom of the image. < IMG ALIGN = MIDDLE SRC = "example.gif" > would align the top of the image example. gif with the middle of the line of text. < IMG ALIGN = BOTTOM SRC = "example.gif" > would align the top of the image example. gif with the bottom of the line of text. In addition, in newer browsers, the following command allows the graphic to be right-aligned on the page, < IMG ALIGN = RIGHT SRC = "example. gif" > . The image example.gif would be placed on the right-hand side of the screen. If the text wraps, it will not drop to the bottom of the image, but will wrap normally. < CENTER > < IMG SRC = "example.gif" > < /CENTER > would center an image, since the ALIGN = CENTER command is still not a standard.

- *Border:* Newer browsers allow commands to determine the thickness of the hyperlink line surrounding an image used as a link. < IMG BORDER = x SRC = "example.gif" > ; the image example.gif would have a border x pixels wide. A setting of 0 will eliminate the hyperlink border. This is useful if your GIF file has a transparent background or when a big blue square around the image would harm the overall design of the page.
- *Height and Width:* These commands determine the dimensions of an image: < IMG HEIGHT = x WIDTH = y SRC = "example. gif" > . The image example.gif would be displayed as x pixels high and y pixels wide. This is useful when an image is larger than you desire for your page. Making an image too small, however, sometimes eliminates the transparent background on some GIF files.

Sample HTML Page with Images

< HTML >
< HEAD >
< TITLE > This Is an HTML Document with Images < /TITLE >
< /HEAD >
< BODY >
< IMG SRC = "example.gif" > Here is a standard image. It is left-justified, and the text will flow from the bottom right-hand corner of the image.
< BR >
< IMG ALIGN = RIGHT SRC = "example.gif" > If using newer brows-

129

ers, this image will be right-justified. Text will begin adjacent to the top of the image and will wrap around to the following lines.
< BR >
< CENTER >Here is a centered image. < BR >
< IMG SRC = "example.gif" > < BR >
This text will also be centered. < /CENTER >
< BR >
< A HREF = "newfile.html" > < IMG SRC = "example.gif" > < /A >Here is an image used as a link to the file newfile.html.
< BR >
< A HREF = "newfile.html" > < IMG BORDER = 0 SRC = "example.gif" > < /A > Here is the same image used as a link to the same file, but with no distinctive hyperlink border.
< /BODY >
< HTML >

HTML-Coded Character Set

The following is from the HTML 2.0 specification, by Tim Berners-Lee and Daniel Connolly, August, 8, 1995. This list details the code positions and characters of the HTML document character set, specified in 9.5, "SGML Declaration for HTML."

&#00;–&#08;	*Unused*
&#09;	Horizontal tab
&#10;	Line feed
&#11;–	Unused
&#13;	Carriage return
&#14;–&#31;	*Unused*
&#32;	Space
&#33;	Exclamation mark (!)
&#34;	Quotation mark (")
&#35;	Number sign (#)
&#36;	Dollar sign ($)
&#37;	Percent sign (%)
&#38;	Ampersand (&)
&#39;	Apostrophe (')
&#40;	Left parenthesis

&#41;	Right parenthesis
&#42;	Asterisk (*)
&#43;	Plus sign (+)
&#44;	Comma (,)
&#45;	Hyphen (-)
&#46;	Period (full stop) (.)
&#47;	Solidus (slash) (/)
0-9	Digits 0-9
&#58;	Colon (:)
&#59;	Semicolon (;)
&#60;	Less than (<)
&#61;	Equals sign (=)
&#62;	Greater than (>)
&#63;	Question mark (?)
&#64;	Commercial at (@)
A-Z	Letters A-Z
&#91;	Left square bracket ([)
&#92;	Reverse solidus (backslash) (\)
&#93;	Right square bracket (])
&#94;	Caret (^)
&#95;	Horizontal bar (underscore) (_)
&#96;	Acute accent (´)
a-z	Letters a-z
&#123;	Left curly brace ({)
|	Vertical bar (|)
&#125;	Right curly brace (})
&#126;	Tilde (~)
&#127;-Ÿ	*Unused*
	Nonbreaking space
&#161;	Inverted exclamation (¡)
&#162;	Cent sign (¢)
&#163;	British Pound Sign (£)
&#164;	General currency sign
&#165;	Yen sign (¥)
&#166;	Broken vertical bar
&#167;	Section sign (§)
&#168;	Umlaut (diaeresis) (¨)
&#169;	Copyright (©)

&#170;	Feminine ordinal (ª)
&#171;	Left angle quote, guillemet left («)
&#172;	Not sign (¬)
&#173;	Soft hyphen
&#174;	Registered trademark (™)
&#175;	Macron accent (^
&#176;	Degree sign (°)
&#177;	Plus or minus (±)
&#178;	Superscript two (²)
&#179;	Superscript three (³)
&#180;	Acute accent (´)
&#181;	Micro sign (µ)
&#182;	Paragraph sign (¶)
&#183;	Middle dot (•)
&#184;	Cedilla
&#185;	Superscript one (¹)
&#186;	Masculine ordinal (º)
&#187;	Right angle quote, guillemet right (»)
&#188;	Fraction one-fourth (¼)
&#189;	Fraction one-half (½)
&#190;	Fraction three-fourths (¾)
&#191;	Inverted question mark (¿)
&#192;	Capital A, grave accent (À)
&#193;	Capital A, acute accent (Á)
&#194;	Capital A, circumflex accent (Â)
&#195;	Capital A, tilde (Ã)
&#196;	Capital A, diaeresis or umlaut mark (Ä)
&#197;	Capital A, ring (Å)
&#198;	Capital AE dipthong (ligature) (Æ)
&#199;	Capital C, cedilla (Ç)
&#200;	Capital E, grave accent (È)
&#201;	Capital E, acute accent (É)
&#202;	Capital E, circumflex accent (Ê)
&#203;	Capital E, diaeresis or umlaut mark (Ë)
&#204;	Capital I, grave accent (Ì)
&#205;	Capital I, acute accent (Í)
&#206;	Capital I, circumflex accent (Î)
&#207;	Capital I, diaeresis or umlaut mark (Ï)

&#208;	Capital Eth, Icelandic
&#209;	Capital N, tilde (Ñ)
&#210;	Capital O, grave accent (Ò)
&#211;	Capital O, acute accent (Ó)
&#212;	Capital O, circumflex accent (Ô)
&#213;	Capital O, tilde (Õ)
&#214;	Capital O, diaeresis or umlaut mark (Ö)
&#215;	Multiplication sign (×)
&#216;	Capital O, slash (Ø)
&#217;	Capital U, grave accent (Ù)
&#218;	Capital U, acute accent (Ú)
&#219;	Capital U, circumflex accent (Û)
&#220;	Capital U, diaeresis or umlaut mark (Ü)
&#221;	Capital Y, acute accent (Ý)
&#222;	Capital thorn, Icelandic
&#223;	Small sharp s, German (sz ligature) (ß)
&#224;	Small a, grave accent (à)
&#225;	Small a, acute accent (á)
&#226;	Small a, circumflex accent (â)
&#227;	Small a, tilde (ã)
&#228;	Small a, diaeresis or umlaut mark (ä)
&#229;	Small a, ring (å)
&#230;	Small ae dipthong (ligature) (æ)
&#231;	Small c, cedilla (ç)
&#232;	Small e, grave accent (è)
&#233;	Small e, acute accent (é)
&#234;	Small e, circumflex accent (ê)
&#235;	Small e, diaeresis or umlaut mark (ë)
&#236;	Small i, grave accent (ì)
&#237;	Small i, acute accent (í)
&#238;	Small i, circumflex accent (î)
&#239;	Small i, diaeresis or umlaut mark (ï)
&#240;	Small eth, Icelandic
&#241;	Small n, tilde (ñ)
&#242;	Small o, grave accent (ò)
&#243;	Small o, acute accent (ó)
&#244;	Small o, circumflex accent (ô)
&#245;	Small o, tilde (õ)

&#246;	Small o, dieresis or umlaut mark (ö)
&#247;	Division sign (÷)
&#248;	Small o, slash (ø)
&#249;	Small u, grave accent (ù)
&#250;	Small u, acute accent (ú)
&#251;	Small u, circumflex accent (û)
&#252;	Small u, diaeresis or umlaut mark (ü)
&#253;	Small y, acute accent (ý)
&#254;	Small thorn, Icelandic
&#255;	Small y, diaeresis or umlaut mark (ÿ)

Common Color Names

Originally picked as being the standard sixteen colors supported by the Windows VGA color palette, these names can be used instead of the hexadecimal codes to specify colors in the BODY and FONT COLOR commands in newer versions of Netscape Navigator and Microsoft Internet Explorer. In addition, four "dark" colors are also supported.

Aqua	Darkred	Olive
Black	Fuchsia	Purple
Blue	Gray	Red
Darkblue	Green	Silver
Darkgray *(appears as light gray)*	Lime	Teal
	Maroon	White
Darkgreen	Navy	Yellow

Hexadecimal Color Codes

The following is list of hexadecimal codes for various colors. The hexadecimal code is used in the BODY and FONT COLOR commands to determine the page background color, the font color, and the color of hyperlinked text. Note: Do not put spaces between the numbers in HTML documents.

A EB D7	Antique white
32 BF C1	Aquamarine

F0 FF FF	Azure	CC CC CC	Gray 4
F5 F5 DC	Beige	00 FF 00	Green
00 00 00	Black	00 80 00	Green *(less yellow)*
FF EB CD	Blanched almond	AD FF 2F	Green yellow
00 00 FF	Blue	F0 FF F0	Honeydew
8A 2B E2	Blue-violet	FF 69 B4	Hot pink
A5 2A 2A	Brown	6B 39 39	Indian red
DE B8 87	Burlywood	FF FF F0	Ivory
5F 92 9E	Cadet blue	B3 B3 7E	Khaki
7F FF00	Chartreuse	E6 E6 FA	Lavender
D2 69 1E	Chocolate	7C FC 00	Lawn green
FF D6 56	Coral	FF FA CD	Lemon
22 22 98	Cornflower blue	B0 E2 FF	Light blue
FF F8 DC	Cornsilk	F0 80 80	Light coral
00 FF FF	Cyan	E0 FF FF	Light cyan
00 56 2D	Dark green	EE DD 82	Light goldenrod
BD B7 6B	Dark khaki	A8 A8 A8	Light gray
55 56 2F	Dark olive green	FF B6 C1	Light pink
FF 8C 00	Dark orange	FF A0 7A	Light salmon
80 00 80	Dark purple	20 B2 AA	Light sea green
E9 96 7A	Dark salmon	87 CE FA	Light sky blue
8F BC 8F	Dark sea green	84 70 FF	Light slate blue
38 4B 66	Dark slate blue	7C 98 D3	Light steel blue
2F 4F 4F	Dark slate gray	FF FF E0	Light yellow
00 A6 A6	Dark turquoise	00 80 00	Lime
94 00 D3	Dark violet	00 AF 14	Lime green
FF 14 93	Deep pink	FA F0 E6	Linen
00 BF FF	Deep sky blue	FF 00 FF	Magenta
8E 23 23	Firebrick	8F 00 52	Maroon
FF FA F0	Floral white	80 00 00	Maroon *(more red)*
50 9F 69	Forest green	00 93 8F	Medium aquamarine
FF 00 FF	Fuchsia	32 32 CC	Medium blue
F8 F8 FF	Ghost white	32 81 4B	Medium forest green
DA AA 00	Gold	D1 C1 66	Medium goldenrod
EF DF 84	Goldenrod	BD 52 BD	Medium orchid
33 33 33	Gray 1	93 70 DB	Medium purple
66 66 66	Gray 2	34 77 66	Medium sea green
99 99 99	Gray 3	6A 6A 8D	Medium slate blue

23 8E 23	Medium spring green	41 68 E1	Royal blue
00 D2 D2	Medium turquoise	8B 45 13	Saddle brown
D5 20 79	Medium violet red	E9 96 7A	Salmon
2F 2F 64	Midnight blue	F4 A4 60	Sandy brown
F5 FF FA	Mint	52 95 84	Sea green
FF E4 E1	Misty rose	FF F5 EE	Seashell
FF E4 B5	Moccasin	96 52 2D	Sienna
FF DE AD	Navajo white	C0 C0 C0	Silver
00 00 80	Navy	72 9F FF	Sky blue
23 23 75	Navy blue	7E 88 AB	Slate blue
FD F5 E6	Old lace	70 80 90	Slate gray
6B 8E 23	Olive	FF FA FA	Snow
80 80 00	Olive *(less yellow)*	41 AC 41	Spring green
FF 87 00	Orange	54 70 AA	Steel blue
FF 45 00	Orange red	DE B8 87	Tan
EF 84 EF	Orchid	00 80 80	Teal
EE E8 AA	Pale goldenrod	D8 BF D8	Thistle
73 DE 78	Pale green	FF 63 47	Tomato
AF EE EE	Pale turquoise	19 CC DF	Turquoise
DB 70 93	Pale violet red	9C 3E CE	Violet
FF DA B9	Peach	F5 DE B3	Wheat
FF B5 C5	Pink	FF FF FF	White
C5 48 98	Plum	F5 F5 F5	White smoke
B0 E0 E6	Powder blue	FF FF 00	Yellow
A0 20 F0	Purple	32 D8 56	Yellow green
FF 00 00	Red		

Recommended Sources

net.Genesis and Devra Hall, *Build a Web Site.* Prima Publishing, Rocklin, California, 1995.

Brent Heslop and Larry Budnick, *HTML Publishing on the Internet.* Ventana Press, Chapel Hill, North Carolina, 1995. (Includes CD-ROM Online Companion.)

Lemay, Laura. *Teach Yourself Web Publishing with HTML in 14 Days,* Premier Edition. Sams.net Publishing, Indianapolis, Indiana, 1995.

Lemay, Laura. *Teach Yourself Web Publishing with HTML in a Week.* Sams.net Publishing. Indianapolis, Indiana, 1995.

Glossary

To help the novice navigate the unfamiliar waters of the Internet, I have compiled a list of essential, informative, and amusing terms common to global networking. Before I begin in alphabetical order let's start with the word *Internet*.

The Internet: The common name for a global collection of interlinked computer networks all using the same communication protocol (see TCP/IP). Commonly known as the Net.

Must-Know Net Glossary

ARPANet: The Internet's direct ancestor. It began operation in 1969 with money from the U.S. Defense Department's Advanced Research Projects Agency (DARPA).

ASCII (American Standard Code Information Interchange): Knowing about ASCII, or at least that it exists, is handy for sending text over the Internet in some cases. This is the de facto worldwide standard for the code numbers that are employed by computers to designate all upper- and lowercase Latin letters, numbers, punctuation, etc.

Backbone: This is the high-speed line or set of connections that is the major framework for data transmission within a network. The Internet is a network of networks that use a variety of backbones maintained by different organizations, both academic and commercial.

Bandwidth: The bandwidth of your Internet connection determines the amount of data that can be sent over the line. Standard copper-wire telephone connections have the lowest bandwidth and fiber optics the highest. Bandwidth, which can also mean the capacity to transmit or absorb information, is used to describe both computer systems and people. Low-bandwidth folks can be easily spotted by the flashing 12:00 on their VCRs.

Baud: The baud rate of a modem indicates the speed of transmission in terms of bits per second it transmits.

BBS (bulletin board system): The equivalent of a hallway bulletin board in electronic format wherein notes and other material are posted in a common forum.

Bit (binary digit): Expressed as either a one or a zero, the bit is the smallest unit of computerized data.

BPS (bits per second): This is the measurement of data speed from one computer location to another, e.g., a 28,800 modem can move data at a rate of 28,800 bits per second.

Browser: The chief client software used for using the Internet, a browser allows you to read the material—text or graphics—that is on the World Wide Web. Currently the most popular browser is Netscape Navigator.

Byte: Eight bits make up a byte's worth of data.

Chat Room: A common area in cyberspace where people meet to discuss and chat.

Client: This is a software application that allows for extracting a variety of "services" for a server computer, such as having a browser, e-mail, or FTP client, each of which allows you to use these respective services from a network server computer.

Clipper Chip: A government-sponsored plan for telecommunications encryption. While signals would automatically be encrypted, the Feds would keep a master list of decryption keys.

Cyberspace: The environment that exists within a global computer network and the place where discussion, news, and events happen in the online world. Coined by William Gibson in his 1984 novel *Neuromancer*, the term has spawned new suffixes and prefixes—cyberpunks and gopherspace, to name a couple.

DNS (domain name system): This is the distributed database system whereby domain names such as cogsum.com are translated into IP numbers, or vice versa. When surfing the Net, you may occasionally receive a DNS error message about a Net page or document that you may have been trying to access. In essence, this means that the Net address that you have been using is wrong or that the page or document has been taken offline.

E-mail (electronic mail): A form of asynchronous communication on the Internet and other networks, such that the recipient does not have to be online at the time the message is sent. Also used as a remote information distribution system—an e-mail server. The e-mail application was one of the first and greatest usages (in volume and usefulness) of the Internet, and remains as one of the chief functions of the Net.

FAQs (frequently asked questions): A list of these questions, posted regularly in Usenet Newsgroups and in the FTP site rfm.mit.edu, seeks to answer inquiries for new Internet users before they are asked. Reading the FAQ is a good way to avoid getting flamed.

Flame: To "yell" at someone or otherwise criticize them online. Flaming e-mail is often distinguished by the use of CAPITAL letters and exclamation marks!!!

Gopher: This aptly named rodent client utility is the best way to negotiate the Net if you have a text-based connection. It enables you to browse through a large series of interconnected menus.

GIF (graphics interchange format): The most common type of image file found on the net. Limited to 256 colors, it is gradually being supplanted by the 24-bit Joint Photographic Experts Group (JPEG) compression format, which allows smaller file sizes.

Host: This is a computer on the Internet that acts as the repository for services that can be used by other computers connecting to the host. The host computer is where a home page is geographically situated and can be located.

HTTP (hypertext transport protocol, a.k.a. hypertext transfer protocol): This is the protocol whereby the Web works using hypertext links that act to connect files across the entire Internet.

ISDN (integrated services digital network): In essence, a digital phone line (versus an analog line) that allows for much greater bandwidth and a consequent reduction in the amount of time spent downloading documents from the Net. Bell Atlantic and other "Baby Bells" are equipped to provide this type of connection to businesses and homes. The cost for such as connection has been decreasing.

Keyword: Usually utilized when performing a keyword search while using one of the various Internet search engines. The majority of indexing by the engines is done with keywords, so, in essence, when one is information hunting for certain subject matter (animal, vegetable, or mineral), one employs a word that is relevant to or within the subject at hand to find a useful citation or reference on the Net.

Mail Bomb: The punishment of choice for serious violators of the rules of behavior on the Usenet. A mail bomb is a huge e-mail message that clogs a perpetrator's host system. When hundreds of mail bombs deluge a system, it can cause a computer to crash. Similarly, a fax bomb sends an endless sheet of black paper to the victim's fax, consuming the paper supply or burning out the machine.

Mosaic: One of the original browser software clients for navigating the World Wide Web, which can be reached if you have a graphics-based Internet connection. A Windows-type program, Mosaic is pretty cool looking, but has long since been outstripped by the Netscape series of browsers.

Modem: Fast becoming one of the chief pieces of computer equipment in the tail end of the century, the modem is that particular computer peripheral used to allow a computer to connect to the phone systems (or other types of data lines) and then to other computers or computer networks, most notably the Internet. The term comes from an amalgam of the words *modulator* and *demodulator,* which describes how the modem works.

Multimedia: A CD-ROM or document on the World Wide Web that combines text, pictures, sound, and video, or any two of these media.

Netiquette: The unofficial rules of etiquette on the Internet. Small violations often result in flaming, while more serious offenses risk incurring a mail-bomb attack.

Net.god: An old-timer in the net.world. One who remembers when the Net was only two computers and a piece of string.

Netscape: This is currently the most popular browser software utilized in surfing the Net and accounts for anywhere from 75 to 85 percent of browsers used to access the World Wide Web. It is so widely employed that many people apply the term *Netscape* in a generic sense in the same way the trademark name *Rollerblade* has come to describe inline skates.

Netsurfer: One who cruises the waves of the Net perpetually looking for new spots to get his or her feet wet. Also used as a term for connecting to the Net just for the thrill of exploration. Often referred to simply as "surfing."

Newbie: A Net newcomer. A derogatory term used by old-timers who resent the use of resources by an ever-expanding population of network novices. Most common usage includes expression like "clueless newbie."

Packet: The Internet breaks up data traveling to and from different Net sites into packets that are bundles of data, each assigned a numbered identity and a relevant Net address. Thus, the way the Net operates is known as *packet switching*.

Server: This term is used interchangeably to designate the software that is used on one particular computer of a network, which allows that computer to offer a service to another computer, such as sending a file upon command. The term can also be used to describe the computer upon which the server software resides. The server responds to client software in rendering a requested service.

Snail Mail: This derogatory term is used to emphasize the difference between e-mail and traditional hard-copy mail. The term is often particularly used to single out mail that is delivered by the post office.

Spamming: To send out multiple nongermane postings on the Usenet. To post messages that have nothing to do with the affected Newsgroups is a cardinal net.sin. The response can be severe. See *mail bomb.*

Slip/PPP (serial line Internet protocol/point-to-point protocol): This is one of the several methods for connecting directly to the Net over the phone.

Smiley: This is the smiling face used as punctuation in e-mail missives. The smiley and other similar types of emotional emphasis in e-mail are known as "emoticons."

Telnet: A way of tapping into a remote computer—as if directly connected—in order to access its publicly available files.

TCP/IP (transmission control protocol/Internet protocol): This is the shared language of all computers on the Net.

Timeout: A timeout is when two computers that are connected over a network—such as the Internet—loose the connection because one of the computers fails to respond over a set time period.

Usenet: This is the oftentimes anarchic arrangement of computer systems that exchange so-called news (individual message postings) among the Newsgroups. A great deal of the Usenet intersects with the Internet at large.

URL (uniform resource locator): Quite simply, the URL of a Web site is its address on the Internet. The most common protocol used in URLs is the hypertext transfer protocol (HTTP) such that most Net addresses start with the *http://* and then continue on into the particular domain and file for which you may be searching. URLs can also be expressed as *FTP://* or as *gopher://* for Net documents that are archived within those respective protocols.

Username: This is the name that you use to log on to a computer system or network (such as the Net) and it is also often used as your e-mail name.

World Wide Web (a.k.a. WWW): This is the most organized facet of the Net by virtue of a series of interconnected pages which include text, graphics, sound, and video.

■

Internet Basics

Getting Connected

It's easy to get connected to the Internet—a simple telephone call will get you online—but it's difficult deciding which kind of a connection is best for you. There are literally hundreds of local, regional, and national companies willing to sign you up to the Internet for a fee. It's as if you had to choose between more than two thousand phone companies when you moved to a new community and were putting in telephone service for the first time.

There are several simple guideposts you can follow to make the decision easy. If you are brand new to the Internet, the best course is to sign up with one of the big commercial online services. These services make the process simple, provide a lot of help to novice Net-surfers and throw in vast amounts of informative and entertaining content from their own resources. There are currently four big commercial online services: America Online, Prodigy, the Microsoft Network, and CompuServe. Costs are similar for each and you can remain with a commercial online service indefinitely under new bulk-rate pricing plans they have adopted.

If you are already comfortable with the Internet, as a result of college experience or a workplace connection, you will probably want to sign up with an Internet service provider (ISP), where you will get competitive rates and reliable service. There are several thousand ISPs around the nation. They have powerful computer servers and multiple phone lines for subscribers. Costs vary from $15 to $30 per month for unlimited time on the Internet. It's important to deal with a direct provider that you can reach with a local phone call; otherwise, your phone bill will go through the roof as you start making heavy use of the Internet. Beware of providers that offer to connect you through a toll-free number, because there is usually a hefty surcharge.

There are local, regional, and national ISPs. All will hook you up to the Internet, but quality of the service and customer support varies widely. Check local newspaper advertisements or the Yellow Pages to find local Internet service providers.

How do you tell the difference between the good and the poor Internet service providers? Check with friends about the ISP they use. Various organizations provide ISP ratings, which are useful to consumers. These can be found in the Internet books that line the shelves at your local bookstore, or online. The online magazine *CNET* published a detailed article on providers in late 1996 and included ratings of some five hundred ISPs, which had been made by Netsurfers who used them. In order, the top ten ISPs listed by *CNET* were:
- NTR.Net Corporation
- Epoch Network
- MindSpring
- Sprint Internet Passport
- IBM Internet Connection
- USA NET
- AT&T WorldNet
- UUNet
- InfiNet

CNET gave its own reviews to many ISPs. Among the providers reviewed was MindSpring, a national company, with more than 100,000 subscribers and 235 locations where it can be reached with a local phone call. The company is dedicated to customer service, and technical support phones are open seven days a week from 9 A.M. to 6 P.M. There are various pricing schedules, including $19.95 monthly for unlimited hours.

Another provider reviewed by *CNET* was AT&T WorldNet, which stunned the Internet world in the spring of 1996 when it offered Internet access free for five hours a month for one year to existing AT&T long-distance subscribers. Unlimited use costs $19.95 per month. A local call will connect you to the Internet in 200 communities and there is toll-free, round-the-clock customer service seven days a week. AT&T WorldNet, which comes bundled with the Netscape Navigator Browser, signed up more than 500,000 subscribers during its first six months.

In addition to listing the top ten ISPs, the *CNET* article listed the ten that received the lowest grades from Netsurfers who took part in the online survey. The worst grade was received by WOW, the kid-oriented discount service offered by CompuServe, which has since been discontinued. Low grades were also received by America Online, Prodigy, and CompuServe. Among them, these three have more than ten million subscribers and the low grade in the *CNET* survey probably reflects the gripes of disgruntled customers among that huge subscriber bases. A major problem mentioned by those in the survey is the computer slowdown at hours of peak usage by subscribers.

There are several sites on the World Wide Web that list hundreds of ISPs geographically and provide a quick rundown on rates and services offered by each provider. The most complete directory of Internet service providers is maintained by Mecklermedia and called, simply, The List. It is located at this Web address: *http://thelist.iworld.com.*

Another comprehensive ISP directory is maintained by the Celestin Company and its address is: *http://www.celestin.com/pocia/.*

Hardware

Almost any computer and modem can be used to connect to the Internet. But, as in all things in the computer world, bigger and faster are better.

A bare-bones rig that will enable you to use the Internet and the graphics-rich World Wide Web to gather information, contact sources, and tap into government data should include the following: a computer with at least a 486 chip, a 250 to 500 megabyte (MB) hard disk, 8 megabytes of memory (RAM), a 14,400 baud modem, and a Web browser such as Netscape Navigator or Microsoft Explorer. That's enough to let you surf around the Internet, gather information, send and receive e-mail, and plug into Usenet Newsgroups.

If you are addicted to Windows 95, you will need a more powerful rig, of course. The 486 chip will do the job, but a Pentium would be best along with 16 megabytes of RAM; a bigger hard disk, which will allow you to store more Internet material; and a 28.8 baud modem.

A stripped-down system will get you on the Net, but, like a 1960 Volkswagen Beetle, an underpowered system will leave you hugging the right-hand shoulder of the information superhighway. Most new computers purchased today will come equipped with everything you need to venture into cyberspace in style.

Commercial Online Services

Here is how to contact the big commercial online services that provide subscribers with Internet access. Rates change frequently in this highly competitive field, and those quoted are for purposes of comparison only. Most offer unlimited time on the Net for $19.95 per month.

- America Online: Call 1-800-827-6364 for a free start-up kit that entitles you to ten hours on line without charge.
- CompuServe: Call 1-800-848-8199 to arrange a one-month introductory membership with ten free hours.
- Prodigy: Call 1-800-776-3449 to learn about its free, one-month, trial membership that includes ten hours on line.
- Microsoft Network: When software giant Microsoft introduced Windows 95 it included a new commercial online service called the Microsoft Network (MSN), which can be used to connect to the Internet. You connect to it directly from Windows 95.

Consumer's Guide to Providers

The Internet's soaring popularity for effecting research, making contacts, conducting interviews, and exchanging e-mail makes an Internet connection almost mandatory these days. But how do you choose from the many providers? There are several questions you should ask any potential Internet access provider before you write that check, according to respected providers we have interviewed.

Question One: Who answers the phone?

The most important item in determining the worth of a provider is whether or not there is someone available to take your calls during business hours. Services run by answering machines indicate that the business may be a sideline for the owner, which does not bode well for the new user or for those with questions or complaints that must be addressed quickly. Long waits or leaving messages because no one is available are also bad signs if they occur regularly. Your provider should also be within your local dialing area.

Question Two: What services are offered?

At the very least, you should demand the following services from any provider: e-mail, Usenet discussion groups, FTP, telnet, gopher, access to the World Wide Web, plus the ability to upload and download files from your home computer. You should also find out how much space your account includes for storing files on the server: 5 MB is the most common limit; 2 MB is probably not enough, especially if you are going to put your own home page on the Web.

Question Three: How many phone lines are available?

One of the most common complaints from Internet account holders is the constant busy signals that plague some providers. Find out the ratio of users-to-phone lines for each company; eight to one is good, while ratios above twelve to one greatly reduce your chance of reliably finding an open line. Also make sure the provider can support at least a 28.8 kbps connection.

Question Four: How is the provider connected to the Internet?

If system performance is a concern, make sure the provider has at least a 256 kbps connection, with either a T1 or T3 line preferred. Also ask what kind of workstation the company uses as its primary server; if it's a PC, you might want to look elsewhere as the smaller personal systems can be overwhelmed by loads that are handled easily by the more powerful SparcStation 10s, SparcStation 20s, and an HP server line.

Question Five: Is live technical support available, at least during business hours?

A corollary to Question One is the willingness of your provider to help you through the problems you encounter while using its service. You should certainly purchase a basic Internet reference work (we recommend *The Whole Internet User's Guide and Catalog*, second edition), but a provider's willingness to make someone available to answer your questions, handle your comments or complaints, and steady your nerves is a major plus.

Question Six: What do you do to protect my privacy?

No system administrator worthy of the name would leave a system open to hackers, but even the most clever techniques can be defeated by a determined attacker. Ensure that your provider does not leave sensitive personal information (such as credit card numbers, phone numbers, or addresses) on the system where they could be discovered. You might also inquire whether the company sells its mailing list to information brokers and what steps need to be taken so that your entry is excluded from the list if you so desire.

Question Seven: How much does all this cost?

Assuming that the provider answers all of your questions satisfactorily, make sure that the price is both reasonable and predictable (no hidden charges). Look for the following items:

- Flat rate, unlimited-time access. Most providers allow their users to stay online as long as they care to with no hourly charge, though if the amount of time included per day is sufficient (at least four hours), this requirement may be modified. In the Washington, D.C., area, $20 per month is average for an unlimited account, though you can often get discounts by signing up for a year at a time.
- No start-up fee.
- No surcharge for using particular services, especially e-mail or the World Wide Web.
- A refund or cancellation policy should you move or decide to discontinue your business with this provider.
- A written contract with a system-use policy and charging plan explained in plain language.

If all of these questions can be answered to your satisfaction, ask for a trial period of not less than five days so you can test and evaluate the system. If it works as expected, you have probably found the provider for you. Of course, you should stay in touch with the provider to let it know if it is falling short of your expectations or if it is continuing to provide good access and support.

An ISDN Connection

If you want to go first-class, you can connect to the Internet through an Integrated Services Digital Network, or ISDN for short. Essentially, it's a souped-up telephone line (digital versus analog) that allows Internet connections at about four times the speed of the fast 28.8 baud modems.

An ISDN line is ordered from your local telephone company, and such service is available in about 70 percent of the country. The cost averages $30 per month. There is also a modest cents-per-minute fee charged for actual usage, like making a long-distance call.

If you invest in an ISDN line, you still need an Internet provider that has the technology to handle such a high-speed hookup. You also need several special pieces of hardware attached to your computer, which take the place of your modem. For this, you get blazing speed on the Internet. No long waits for graphics-rich pages to load. Swift downloads of data. Be warned, however; ISDN lines are very difficult to set up and configure.

The Internet on TV

A new generation of electronic devices enable users to Netsurf on their living-room television sets. They are small boxes which rest atop the TV set, cost about $300, and are sold in electronic stores.

For about $20 per month, the set-top Internet box gives you unlimited time on the Internet, with a wireless keyboard used to navigate and the results displayed on the TV set. The actual Internet connection is made with a modem built into the box and hooked to your family phone line. Initial reviews of this "Web TV" setup have been positive.

A Cable Modem

Now that we have informed you of the availability and the speed of ISDN lines, you should also be informed that ISDNs and other slower types of connections may become obsolete within a few years because of incredibly fast cable modems. These hookups to the Net promise to deliver the full science fiction–like effect of cyberspace that is often written about when one reads about the information superhighway.

For starters, you will be able to get real-time video feeds over the Net, so you will be able to order movies from vast data banks, and also cable modems will herald the beginning of the first interactive television. But the possibilities aren't limited to just the parochial purpose of watching movies and interactive TV over the Net. Everything that is accessible over the Internet will be delivered all the faster.

The cable modems undergoing testing currently operate up to one thousand times faster than a 14,400-bits-per-second modem. Under regular modem speed, for instance, it takes around eighteen hours to download Windows 95 software via the Internet, but with a cable modem this could be done in about a minute.

Several commercial organizations—including Tell-Communications Inc., Time Warner, Comcast, and Continental Cablevision—have begun offering cable modems in a few markets, but their plans are not yet set in stone. And it will be a while yet until this type of hookup is available across the country.

Navigating the Net—A Guide to Understanding URLs

For those just entering the Internet, the lengthy Net site addresses that are used can seem confusing. You may ask: Why are they so long? Why are some longer than others? But once you understand how to read and use addresses—URLs in particular—you will be able to navigate the Internet with relative ease and speed.

Any Internet address is comprised of several components: For URLs, the part that comes after the *http://* consists of the host name, the directory path, and a file name. Remember, anything with the prefix *http* means that a particular site is located on a World Wide Web server. Here's the URL for the home page of *The Internet Newsroom,* my monthly newsletter publication: *http://www2.dgsys.com/~editors/index.html.*

The */www2.dgsys.com/* is the host name, and the */~editors/* is the directory path, and the *index.html* is the file name. By the way, the little " ~ " is known as the tilde, but you don't see it in too many addresses.

Many lengthy addresses you will encounter appear as such because they have a long set of *subpaths* after the original directory path. Here's an example of how to reach the opening lines of Hamlet on the Internet, which involves several subpaths: *http://www.mindsprings.com/ ~hamlet/hamlet/hamlet11.html*.

The */~hamlet/* is the directory path, and all the *hamlets* after are subpaths to the opening lines.

Browsers

To understand the sudden explosion of the Internet and the rapid growth of the Net's most popular part—the World Wide Web—it is necessary to understand the history of Mosaic, the first Web browser to come into use.

A browser allows an Internet user to easily access and download the informative multimedia documents available on the World Wide Web. The Web was created in 1991 by scientists at the European Particle Physics Laboratory (CERN is its French acronym), and its emergence changed everything.

The Web and the invention of Mosaic as a browser made the previously unwieldy Internet user friendly. Previously on the Internet, the only way to navigate this global computer network was by using Unix commands and sifting through rather unattractive text interfaces. While this text-based interface is often still the faster method of traveling on the Net, the Web has made the Internet easy to use and attractive.

With browsing software such as Mosaic or Netscape, all a Net navigator need do is point-and-click the mouse onto a highlighted or underlined word (a text link), which connects to a document, that can contain text, graphics, video, and even sound. And there is a lot that can be found on the World Wide Web.

This was all made possible because in the search for making the Internet easier, the CERN programmers created a standard for data and a universal addressing system that led not only to an explosion of Internet usage but also to a huge push toward publishing material of all types on the Internet.

Using commands that are relatively simple, anyone can publish material in hypertext, wherein certain parts of a document become a link to yet another document. This creates an effect whereby the Web gets its name—as a seamless flow of information that is intertwined. The beginning point for any Net travel and any particular site is known as a home page and each succeeding link leads to yet more pages. A browser acts as reader of hypertext language.

It did take the invention of browsers such as Mosaic, as a complement to the World Wide Web, to allow for the point-and-click interface that has become so popular. Mosaic was invented at the National Center for Supercomputing Applications (NCSA) at the University of Illinois in early 1993. After a story ran in the *New York Times* about Mosaic, there were more than a thousand people a day flooding the Internet to download Mosaic software made available free by NCSA.

While this client browser software—in its upgraded version—is still available via NCSA, there are also commercially licensed versions available such as the Mosaic software sold by Spry Incorporated under the name Internet-In-A-Box. All the World Wide Web browsers are somewhat derived from the original Mosaic software. And, each of the three big commercial online services—Prodigy, America Online, and CompuServe—now use similar looking browsers to offer Internet access to its subscribers.

The browsers all have a window that one opens to type in the address (URL) of the World Wide Web site he or she wants to reach. If you want to get to a location on the Web, but don't know the address, there are search tools provided that will look it up for you. Once you find a site you like, you can add it to a "Hot List" or bookmark on your browser, where it can be quickly called up at a later time.

Since its inception, the original Mosaic has been superseded by the Netscape Navigator, which was designed by one of the original creators of Mosaic. The Netscape Navigator, produced by Netscape Communications Corp., currently accounts for over 75 percent of the browser software used throughout the Net. Also, the majority of Web pages are designed with "Netscape enhancement" in mind, which means essentially that they are best viewed and read using Netscape Navigator. But this doesn't mean other browsers are obsolete, or no good; there are many out there, and Netsurfers should use the one they like best and are most comfortable using.

E-mail Addresses for Publications

The following is a short list of e-mail addresses for U.S. newspapers, magazines, and other publications that writers may wish to contact to query submission procedures:

Africalink (Philadelphia)	sern@aol.com
AI Expert	76702705@compuserve.com
Albany Times Union	
Assistant managing editor	mspain6581@aol.com
Capitol Bureau	tucapitol@aol.com
Executive editor	jdco@aol.com
General reporters and staff	tunewsroom@aol.com
Letters to the editor	tuletters@aol.com
Library	tulibrary@aol.com
Albion Books (San Francisco)	info@albion.com
Albuquerque Tribune	rbuergi@etrib.com
Allure (New York)	alluremag@aol.com
Anchorage Daily News	742202560@compuserve.com
Arizona Republic	
Assistant managing editor	amycar@aol.com
Assistant features editor	phennessy@aol.com

Features editor	whitejsee@aol.com
Home Buying Choices	hfinberg@pni.com
Home Buying Choices	dgianelli@pni.com
Short Takes editor	dhontz@republicpni.com
Arkansas Democrat-Gazette	
(Little Rock, AR)	news@arkdg.com
Army Times Publishing	armytimes@aol.com
Associated Press	
"On the Net" column only	weise@wellsfcaus.com
Atlanta Journal-Constitution	gpph16a@prodigy.com
Austin Chronicle	xephyr@bga.com
Australian Broadcast	
(Washington, D.C.)	peterryan@delphi.com
Aviation Daily (Washington, D.C.)	grahamg@mgh.com
The Baltimore Sun	baltsun@clark.net
The Bergen Record (Hackensack, NJ)	newsroom@bergen-record.com
Boston Globe	
Arts editor	arts@globe.com
Ask the Globe	ask@globe.com
City Weekly section	ciweek@globe.com
Comments on coverage/	
Ombudsman	ombud@globe.com
Confidential Chat	chat@globe.com
Health & Science section	howwhy@globe.com
Letters to the editor	letter@globe.com
Plugged In	plugged@globe.com
Real Estate section	lots@globe.com
Religion editor	religion@globe.com
Story Ideas	news@globe.com
Submissions to "Voxbox" column	voxbox@globe.com
Thursday Calendar section	list@globe.com
Boston Herald	
Other Op-ed Comments	heraldpol@delphi.com
Political Comments	heraldedit@delphi.com
Boston Phoenix	7163263@compuserve.com
Business Week (Lexington, MA)	bwreader@mgh.com
Cape Cod Times	cctimes@delphi.com
Car and Driver	editors@caranddriver.com

CBS
  Late Show with David Letterman   lateshow@pipeline.com
  News Up to the Minute   mail@uttm.com
Charlotte Observer   garynielson@community.com
Chicago Tribune   tribletter@aol.com
  Deputy Director
    Online Publications   jwcary@suntimes.com
  Director Online Publications   lebolt@suntimes.com
Christian Science Monitor (Op-ed)   oped@rachelcsps.com
Chronicle of Higher Education   cditor@chroniclemerit.edu
Chronicle-Telegram (Elyria, OH)   macroncl@freenetlorainoberlin.edu
City Pages (Minneapolis)   citypages@igcapc.org
City Paper (Philadelphia)   7163257@compuserve.com
City Sun (New York)
  Computer column   sysop@f206n278z1fido.net.org
CNN (Washington, D.C.)
  Global News   cnnglobal@aol.com
Colorado Daily (Boulder, CO)   colorado_daily@one.net-bbs.org
The Columbus Dispatch   crow@cdcolumbus.ohus
  Letters to the editor   letters@cdcolumbus.ohus
.communications News   489-8359@mcimail.com
.communications Week   440-7485@mcimail.com
.community News (Aledo, TX)   .commnews@airmail.net
.computerWorld   letters@cw.com
Congressional Quarterly   hotline@cqalert.com
Connect Magazine   connect@aol.com
Contra Costa County Times (CA)
  Letters to the editor   cctletrs@netcom.com
Conus Washington/TV Direct (D.C.)   conus-dc@clark.net
Cowles/SIMBA Media Daily   simba02@aol.com
Crafts 'n Things (Des Plaines, IL)   725671066@compuserve.com
Crain's Chicago Business   ccbnews@aol.com
C-SPAN (Washington, D.C.)
  Questions during live call-ins   cspanguest@aol.com
  Requests for coverage   cspanprogm@aol.com
  Viewer services and questions   cspanviewr@aol.com
Daily Citizen (Washington, D.C.)   ben@essential.org
Daily Pacific Builder (San Francisco)   dbuilder@aol.com

Daily Pennsylvanian
    (University of Pennsylvania)   dailypenn@a1relayupenn.edu
Daily Texan (U. of Texas-Austin)   texan@utxvmsccutexas.edu
Daytona Beach News-Journal (FL)   721421666@compuserve.com
Dallas Morning News   747742236@compuserve.com
Defense News   766221732@compuserv.com
Democrat-Gazette (Little Rock, AR)   news@arkdg.com
Des Moines Register (IA)   dsmreg@delphi.com
Details (NY)   detailsmag@aol.com
Detroit Free Press
    Business news department   business@det-freepress.com
    City desk   city@det-freepress.com
    Tech columnist   watha@det-freepress.com
Evansville Courier (IN)
    Computer/Internet Columnist   jderk@evansville.net
    General   courier@evansville.net
Fairfax Journal (VA)   journalexp@aol.com
Farmer's Market Online   marketfarm@aol.com
Fayetteville Observer-Times (NC)   frink@infi.net*
Federal Computer Week   letters@fcw.com
Flint Journal (MI)   fj@flintj.com
Forbes   5096930@mcimail.com
Ft. Lauderdale Sun-Sentinel   sbanderson@aol.com
Fox TV (CA)   foxnet@delphi.com
Free Times   71632165@compuserve.com
Galveston County Daily (TX)   galvnews@aol.com
Gazette-Telegraph (Colorado Springs)   gazette@usa.net
Glamour (NY)   glamourmag@aol.com
Government Computer News   editor@gcn.com
GQ (Orlando)   gqmag@aol.com
Hartford Courant   courant@pnet.com
Hollywood Reporter   thrscott@aol.com
Home Office Computing   hoc@aol.com
Home PC   homepc@aol.com
Honolulu Star-Bulletin   davids@aloha.net
Houston Chronicle
    Computing   dwightsilverman@chron.com
    Tank McNamara   760572423@compuserve.com

Houston Chronicle, Electronic Media
 Content manager   jimtownsend@chron.com
 Content coordinator   mikeread@chron.com
 Community content   susanamelton@chron.com
 Daily content   davidgalloway@chron.com
 Sports content   markevangelista@chron.com
 Virtual Voyager   glengolightly@chron.com
Houston Public News   griggs@jetsonuh.edu
Icon (Iowa City)   icon@igcapc.org
Idaho State Journal (Pocatello, ID)
 City/county economy   peterisj@aol.com
 Environment   timisj@aol.com
 Online Czar   isjrep@aol.com
 Press Club   maryisj@aol.com
 State/politics   debisj@aol.com
Idaho Statesman (Boise)   764243356@compuserve.com
The Indiana Daily Student
 (Bloomington)   IDS@opheliaucsindiana.edu
Information Week   informationweek@mcimail.com
Infoworld   letters@infoworld.com
The Innovator (University Park, IL) gsurag@bgu.edu
Inside Media (NY)   mediaseven@aol.com
International Herald-Tribune iht@eurokomie
Internet Business Advantage (Lancaster, PA)
           edit@wentworth.com
The Internet Business Journal mstrange@fonorola.net
The Internet Novice   tates@accessdigex.net
Internet World   neubarth@mecklermedia.com
The Knoxville News-Sentinel
 Newsroom   kns-news@useusit.net
 Letters   kns-letters-to-editor@useusit.net
LA Weekly   laweekly@aol.com
La Crosse Tribune (WI)   712103567@compuserve.com
The Las Vegas Sun (NV)
 Managing editor   thompson@lvsun.com
Leader-Telegram (Eau Claire, WI) jaymar@discover-.netnet
The Ledger-Star (Portsmouth, VA) debg@infi.net
Los Angeles Times

Business editor	business@latimes.com
Business editor	bobmaguson@latimes.com
Deputy editor	billsing@latimes.com
Company Town	marksaylor@latimes.com
Financial Markets	dangaines@latimes.com
Sunday Business	tomfurlong@latimes.com
The Cutting Edge	jonathonweber@latimes.com
MacUser	letters@macuserziff.com
General	info@mactech.com
Press releases	press_releases@mactech.com
MacWeek	letters@macweekziff.com
Mademoiselle (NY)	mllemag@aol.com
Maine Public TV	
Media Watch	greenman@mainemaine.edu
Media Page	mpage@netcom.com
Metropulse (Knoxville, TN)	metropulse@aol.com
Middlesex News (Framingham, MA)	mnews@worldstd.com
Technology editor (Eric Bauer)	ebauer@mnews.com
Minneapolis Star Tribune	
Letters to the editor	opinion@startribune.com
Minnesota politics feedback	politics@startribune.com
Star Tribune Online	roberts@startribune.com
Minnesota Daily	
(University of Minnesota)	network@editmndlyumn.edu
Minnesota News Council	newscncl@mtn.org
Mondo 2000	mondo@well.com
Monitor Publications (AZ)	743532767@compuserve.com
Monitor Radio (Boston)	radio@csps.com
Morning Journal (Lorain, OH)	mamjornl@free.netlorain.oberlin.edu
Mother Jones	x@mojones.com
Ms. (letters to the editor)	ms@echonyc.com
Multimedia Business Report	simba02@aol.com
Multimedia World	753002503@compuserve.com
The Nation	nation@igc.org
National Journal	njcirc@clark.net
National Public Radio (Washington, D.C.)	
Fresh Air	freshair@hslc.org
Letterbox	letterbox@wshbcsms.com

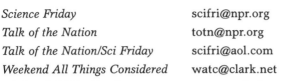

Science Friday	scifri@npr.org
Talk of the Nation	totn@npr.org
Talk of the Nation/Sci Friday	scifri@aol.com
Weekend All Things Considered	watc@clark.net
Weekend Edition/Sunday	wesun@clark.net
West Coast Live	owner-west_coast_live@net.com.com
NBC	
Dateline	dateline@newsnbc.com
Late Night with Conan O'Brien	conanshow@aol.com
NBC News Burbank	glewis@newsnbc.com
Nightly News	nightly@newsnbc.com
Today	today@newsnbc.com
TV Nation	tvnatn@aol.com
NetGuide	netmail@netguidecmp.com
Network Computing	network_computing@mcimail.com
Network World	
General, letters, Cyberspeak	network@worldstd.com
Reader Advocacy Force	nwraf@worldstd.com
New Business Watch (Sebastopol, CA)	70307454@compuserve.com
New England Cable News	
(Needham, MA)	necn@aol.com
The New Republic (Washington, D.C.)	editors@tnr.com
New Scientist, UK (U.S. Bureau)	newscidc@sohoios.com
New York Times	
Business Day	bizday@nytimes.com
Letters to the editor	letters@nytimes.com
Letters to the editor,	
NYT Magazine	magazine@nytimes.com
Media business	
(Monday Business Day)	mediabiz@nytimes.com
Money & Business column	
submissions	mainwall@nytimes.com
	onthejob@nytimes.com
	viewpts@nytimes.com
	yourmind@nytimes.com
New Jersey Weekly	jersey@nytimes.com
Science Times	scitimes@nytimes.com
The Week in Review	review@nytimes.com

for a list of other staff send message to:	staff@nytimes.com
New York Transfer News	nyt@blythe.org
The News Herald (Cleveland, OH)	fi378@clevelandfree.net.edu
The News & Record (Greensboro, NC)	
Letters	edpage@nrinfi.net
Newsbytes	newsbytes@geniegeis.com
Newsweek	
Letters to the editor	letters@newsweek.com
"Periscope"	ghackett@newsweek.com
Northern Star (DeKalb, IL)	star@wpocsoniu.edu
Ohio University Public Television	tv@ohiou.edu
The Olympian (Olympia, WA)	olympian@halcyon.com
Online Access	oamag@aol.com
The Orange County Register (CA)	wilde@ocr1freedom.com
Orlando Sentinel	
Destination Florida	dfjulie@aol.com
OutNOW! (San Jose)	jct@netcom.com
Palo Alto Weekly	paweekly@netcom.com
PBS, "POV" (Washington, D.C.)	povonline@aol.com
PC Computing	7600021@compuserve.com
PC Magazine	
Letters	1579301@mcimail.com
Solutions	5563896@mcimail.com
PC Week	557-0379@mcimail.com
Philadelphia Inquirer	
Editorial page	editpage@aol.com
"Personal Computing" column	reidgold@netaxs.com
Phoenix Gazette	phxgazette@aol.com
The Pilot (Norfolk, VA)	boyer@infi.com
Playboy (Chicago)	edit@playboy.com
Dear Playboy	dearpb@playboy.com
Playboy Forum	forum@playboy.com
Political Science Quarterly (NY)	psq123@aol.com
Popular Communications	
(Hicksville, NY)	pop.comm@aol.com
Popular Science	751401732@compuserve.com
Port Townsend Leader (WA)	leader@ptolympus.net

Portales News-Tribune (NM)	pnt4481@aol.com
Portland Oregonian	oreeditors@aol.com
Prague Post	100120361@compuserve.com
The Progressive (Madison, WI)	progmag@igcapc.org
Public Radio International	
(formerly APR) "Marketplace"	market@usc.edu
Raleigh News & Observer	
Executive editor	frank3@nando.net
Online editor	bsicelof@nando.net
Razorbooks USA (AZ)	743532767@compuserve.com
Reason	707032152@compuserve.com
The Register-Guard (Eugene, OR)	tomd780@aol.com
Assistant city editor	731132774@compuserve.com
Reno Gazette-Journal	rgj@lib.comdps.com
Richmond Times-Dispatch	davechapin@aol.com
Ridgefield Press (CT)	710523315@compuserve.com
The Riverfront Times (St. Louis)	rft@plinkgeis.com
Rolling Stone (NY)	rollingstone@echonyc.com
Rush Limbaugh Show (NY)	702772502@compuserve.com
The Rutland Tribune (Rutland, VT)	ruttrib@vermontel.com
Sacramento Bee (CA)	sacbee@netcom.com
Letters, op-ed pieces	sacbedit@netcom.com
The Sagebrush (U. of Nevada)	sgbrush@shadowscsunr.edu
Salt Lake Tribune	theeditors@sltrib.com
San Diego Daily Transcript	editor@sddt.com
San Diego Union-Tribune	
Bi-weekly Internet section only	computerlink@sduniontrib.com
San Francisco Chronicle	chronletters@sfgate.com
San Francisco Examiner	letters@examiner.com
San Francisco Examiner	sfexaminer@aol.com
San Francisco Examiner Magazine	sfxmag@mcimail.com
Santa Cruz County Sentinel (CA)	
Letters to the editor	sented@cruzio.com
News desk	sentcity@cruzio.com
Saratoga News (CA)	sn@livewire.com
Science	
General editorial inquiries	science_editors@aaas.org
General news	science_news@aaas.org

Letters to the editor	science_letters@aaas.org
Manuscript reviews	science_reviews@aaas.org
Scientific American (NY)	letters@sciam.com
The Shield (U. of Southern Indiana)	jandersoucs@smtpusi.edu
Southwestern Union Record	727341717@compuserve.com
St. Paul Pioneer Press	
Virtual Reality	vpress@aol.com
St. Petersburg Times	731743344@compuserve.com
Star-Telegram (Fort Worth)	mhammond@delphi.com
Stars and Stripes	jenie@wamumd.edu
The State (Columbia, SC)	state@scsn.net
The Stranger (Seattle)	stranger@cyberspace.com
Stuart/St. Lucie News	
(Port St. Lucie, FL)	mdodge1@geniegeis.com
The Sun Times (Chicago)	decc@csuchicago.edu
Sun Newspapers	sun@sunnews.com
Tampa Tribune	
Online editor	sywg06A@prodigy.com
The Tartan	
(Carnegie-Mellon University)	tartan@andrewcmu.edu
Time	timeletter@aol.com
The Times (Munster, IN)	kerr@howpubs.com
Town-Crier (Wellington, FL)	thecrier@magg.net
The Tribune (Chicago)	
Letters to the editor	tribletter@aol.com
The Troubadour (Franciscan Univ.)	741432374@compuserve.com
Tucson Citizen	
Letters to the editor	tcnews@aol.com
Tucson Weekly	
Letters to the editor only	71632105@compuserve.com
Twin Cities Reader (Minneapolis)	sari23@aol.com
Urbana News-Gazette (IL)	gazette@prairie.net.org
U.S. News & World Report	
(Washington, D.C.)	letters@usnews.com
USA Today (Washington, D.C.)	
Letters to the editor	usatoday@clark.net
USA Weekend	usaweekend@aol.com
USF Oracle (Tampa)	

Editor-in-chief	connolly@soleila.compusf.edu
News editor	perez@soleila.compusf.edu
Utne Reader (Minneapolis)	editor@utnereader.com
Valdosta Daily Times (Valdosta, GA)	gambr@wwwvaluu.net
Valley Breeze (Cumberland, RI)	valbreeze@aol.com
Vancouver Columbian (WA)	vanpaper@aol.com
VeloNews (Boulder, CO)	velonews@aol.com
Vibe	vibeonline@nyo.com
The Village Voice (NY)	voice@echonyc.com
The Virtual Times, Huntsville, Alabama Edition	editor@hsv.com
The Virtual Times, International Edition	editor@hsv.com
Vogue (NY)	voguemail@aol.com
Voice of America/WorldNet Television (Washington, D.C.)	
Agriculture Today	agri@voa.gov
From outside the U.S.	letters@voa.gov
From within the U.S.	letters-usa@voa.gov
QSL reports, inside U.S.	qsl-usa@voa.gov
QSL reports, outside U.S.	qsl@voa.gov
VOA-Europe (English)	voa-europe@voa.gov
VOA-Morning Program	voa-morning@voa.gov
Wall Street Journal Subscription services only	wsjservice@cordowjones.com
Washington City Paper (Washington, D.C.)	washcp@aol.com
Wired (CA)	infodroid@wired.com
	editor@wired.com
Women's Wear Daily	wwd@ccabc.com

■

Listservs for Writers

The following writer-relevant Listservs are courtesy of a Web page called Bricolage, created by Trevor Lawrence, which can be found at this URL: *http://bel.avonibp.co. uk/bricolage/resources/lounge/TWRG/index.html*

Booknews

TOPICS: Reviews of upcoming books, CDs, and videos (moderated). SUBSCRIPTION: send e-mail to *LISTSERVER@COLUMBIA.ILC. COM*, subscribe to "booknews yourfirstname yourlastname." POSTING: *BOOKNEWS@COLUMBIA.ILC.COM*

Book-Talk

TOPICS: Discussions and information about new books, CDs, and videos. SUBSCRIPTION: send e-mail to *LISTSERVER@COLUMBIA. ILC.COM*, subscribe to "book-talk yourfirstname yourlastname." POSTING: *BOOK-TALK@COLUMBIA.ILC.COM*

The Composition Digest

TOPICS: "A weekly Newsgroup for the study of computers and writing, specifically writing instruction in computer-based classrooms." SUBSCRIPTION: send e-mail to *listserve@ULKYVX.BITNET*, subscribe to: "subscribe COMPOS01 yourfirstname yourlastname." POSTING: *COMPOS01@ ULKYVX.BITNET*

The Garret

TOPICS: "The Enclave Writers' Network and Support Group mailing list digest." SUBSCRIPTION: send e-mail to *server@nocturne. boulder-creek. ca.us*, "JOIN GARRET yourfirstname yourlastname." POSTING: *garret@ nocturne.boulder-creek.ca.us*

L'atelier Ecrivains

TOPICS: French language list for writers, for criticism of works in progress, and for discussion of writing issues. Participation is required; this is not a place to find reading materials. Subscription by owner only (Rhéal Nadeau or Jean-Claude Boudreault). SUBSCRIPTION: send e-mail to *listserver@uquebec.ca*, subscribe to "sub ecrivains yourfirstname yourlastname." POSTING: *ecrivains@ uquebec.ca.* OWNERS: *nadeau@bnr.ca Jean-Claude_Boudreault@ UQTR.UQuebec.CA*

Media List

TOPICS: "A listing of newspapers, magazines, TV stations, and other media outlets that accept e-mail and electronic submissions." SUBSCRIPTION: send to "subscribe MEDIALIST YourFirstNameYour LastName," in message body to *MAJORDOMO@WORLD.STD. COM.*

Nwu-Chat

TOPICS: A mailing list of the National Writers Union. The list is open to all working writers, with discussion focused on internal union business, shoptalk, industry news, civil liberties, and the labor movement. SUBSCRIPTION: send e-mail to: *LISTSERV@ NETCOM.COM*, subscribe to "subscribe nwu-chat yourfirstname yourlastname." POSTING: *nwu-chat@NETCOM.COM*

Poetry List

TOPICS: "This list is designed to be a forum where original poetry (either complete or in progress) may be posted by members interested in critique-style discussion, examination, and analysis of their work. It is assumed that all members will at some point post an original piece, and not merely assume an exclusively responsive role." SUBSCRIPTION: send e-mail to *listserve@gonzaga.edu*, subscribe to: "subscribe poetry yourfirstname yourlastname." POSTING: *POETRY@GONZAGA.EDU*

Screen Writing Discussion List

TOPICS: "A discussion list of the joy and challenge of screenwriting for film and TV. Any topic of interest to writers or potential writers is appropriate (e.g., format, story ideas, dialogue, characters, agents, producers, directors, actors, studios, problems, and/or solutions)." SUB-SCRIPTION: send e-mail to *listserve@tamvm1.bitnet*, subscribe to: "subscribe scrnwrit yourfirstname yourlastname." POSTING: *SCRNWRIT @TAMVM1.BITNET*

SFNF-Writers

TOPICS: "A mailing list for people interested in writing science fiction and/or fantasy. It is intended for both serious authors and dabblers." SUBSCRIPTION: send e-mail to *majordomo@seidel. ncsa.uiuc.edu*, subscribe to: "subscribe scrnwrit yourfirstname yourlastname." LIST OWNER: *leppik@seidel.ncsa.uiuc.edu*

Small-Press Mailing List

TOPICS: "Concerns of authors and editors involved with the small press, both of books and of magazines. Printers and services, announcements, calls for submissions, bookstores, discussion of acceptance and rejections, book and signing events, readings, 'war stories,' advice for writers, editors, self-publishers." SUBSCRIPTION: send your readable request to join or leave to: *small-press-request@world.std.com*. Posts to the list go to *small-press@world.std. com*. MODERATOR: *ctan@world.std.com* (Cecilia M Tan).

Writer's Workshop

TOPICS: The Writer's list is an open, unmoderated electronic workshop for discussions of the art and craft of writing and sharing of works in progress. As might be expected, writers tend to write quite a lot, so be prepared for plenty of mail. SUBSCRIPTION: The workshop is self-serve. Send e-mail to: *listserv@mitvma.mit.edu* (or *listserv@mitvma. mit.bitnet*) with the message "SUBSCRIBE WRITERS yourfirstname yourlastname."

Writing Center

TOPICS: A discussion list for directors of academic writing centers, including evaluating software for writing instruction, use of tutors, and other issues specific to writing centers. SUBSCRIPTION: Send e-mail to *listserv@TTUVM1.BITNET* with the message "SUBSCRIBE W-CENTER yourfirstname yourlastname." POSTING: *CENTER@TTUVM1.BITNET*

■

Net Resources for Writers

The following is a hand-picked selection of URLs for various writing-related pages, book publishers, style guides, and other Web sites that may prove interesting or useful to you as a wordsmith.

http://www.africaonline.com/
   The African Writer's Series
http://www.tcbi.com/~artex/
   Artex Publishing
http://www.panix.com/~aaww/
   Asian American Writer's Workshop
http://tfnet.ils.unc.edu/~jacobs/index.html
   Aspiring Writers Link
http://www.ozemail.com.au/~awol/
   Australian Writing Online (AWOL)
http://www.authorlink.com
   Authorlink!
http://www.light-communications.com/author/index.html
   Author's Showcase
http://www.whidbey.net/~oneguy/beltowr/bellpage.htm
   Bell Tower Publishing

http://wnc.com/btl.html

    Between the Lines

http://incolor.inetnebr.com/bstarp/

    Black Star Press

http://web.syr.edu/~pdverhey

    Book Arts Web

http://www.polyweb.com/BookBrowser

    BookBrowser, a Guide for Avid Readers

http://www.bookzone.com

    BookZone

http://bel.avonibp.co.uk/bricolage/welcome.html

    Bricolage

http://www.islandnet.com/~caa/other.html

    Canadian Authors Association

http://www.mindspring.com/~cbi/

    Children's Writing Resource Center

http://www.studiob.com

    Computer Book Café

http://www.copyright.com/

    Copyright Clearance Center

http://www.crispzine.com

    Crisp

http://www.ReadersNdex.com/crow

    CROW (Capsule Reviews of Original Work)

http://www.cyberzines.com

    Cyberzines

http://www.echoesmag.com

    Echoes Literary Magazine

http://wings.buffalo.edu/epc/home.html

    The Electronic Poetry Center

http://www.fwl.com/fwl

    Fantasy Writers, Ltd.

http://www.mnet.fr/freecyb/FataMorgana/

    Fata Morgana

http://www.glimmertrain.com

    Glimmer Train Press Short Story Magazine

http://www.mala.bc.ca/~mcneil/template.htx

    Great Books Home Page

http://www.io.org/~gutter/
  Gutter Press
http://.www.dryden.com/dryden.html
  The Harcourt Brace Office Handbook, 6th Edition
http://www.execpc.com/hawes/
  Hawes Publications Books
http://members.aol.com/swbrodie/honey/
  Illya's Honey
http://www.inkspot.com/~ohi/ink/inklings.html
  Inklings
http://sunsite.unc.edu/dykki/poetry/home.html
  Internet Poetry Archive
http://www.spinfo.uni-koeln.de/~dm/eire.html
  Irish Poetry Page
http://www.netdiva.com/isisplus.html
  Isis: Black Women's Art and Culture
http://www.athenet.net/~lavsalon
  The Lavender Salon Reader Online!
http://www.libraria.it
  Libraria via della Giuliana
http://www.tlt.com
  The Literary Times Magazine Online
http://www.tc.umn.edu/nlhome/m555/loft/index.html
  The Loft: A Place for Writing and Literature
http://www.execpc.com/~mbr/bookwatch
  Midwest Book Review
http://www.tale.com/
  Mind's Eye Fiction
http://www.avsi.com/minsky/
  Minsky Online
http://users.aol.com/bryantav/
  Multicultural Writer's Group Home Page
http://www.mysterynet.com
  MysteryNet.com
http://home.earthlink.net/~emfarrell/mythsoc/mythsoc.html
  The Mythopoeic Society
http://www.kiosk.net/poetry/about.html
  National Library of Poetry

http://www.nj.com/arts/Reading

New Jersey Online Arts: The Reading Room

http://www.mysterynew.com

New Mystery Magazine

http://www.albany.edu/writers-inst/

New York State Writers Institute at the State University of New York

http://www.ninc.com

Novelists, Inc.

http://www.purefiction.com/contents.htm

Pure Fiction Interest

http://www.io.com:80/user/aapex/quotations.html

Quotation Resources

http://www.demon.co.uk/review/

The Richmond Review

http://comet.net/romance

The Romance Pages

http://www.romanceweb.com

Romancing the Web

http://www.shout.net/~ccandd

Scars Publications

http://www.sfwa.org/sfwa/

Science Fiction and Fantasy Writers of America, Inc.

http://www.smallpress.com

Small Press and *Publishing Entrepreneur* magazines

http://www.twc.org/

Teachers and Writers Collaborative

http://www.utne.com

Utne Reader and *Utne Reviews*

http://www.wiley.com/

John Wiley & Sons, Inc.

http://www.writepage.com/

The Write Page

http://www.writer.org

The Writer's Center

http://www.writersconf.com

The Writers Conference

http://www.nashville.net/~edge

The Writer's Edge

http://www.womenslink.com

The Writer's Table at Women's Link

http://www.mythbreakers.com/writingschool

The Writing School

http://www.yahoo.com/Arts/Literature/Writing/Institutes/

Yahoo Writing Institutes Index

Author, Author!

The following URLs will lead you to Web pages that pertain to a variety of well-known authors. These are devotional, biographical types of pages, and more important to researchers, many of the Net pages listed here contain the works of the authors mentioned.

http://www.umd.umich.edu/ ~ nhughes/dna/

Adams, Douglas

http://web.msu.edu/lecture/angelou.html

Angelou, Maya

http://www.clark.net/pub/edseiler/WWW/asimov_home_page.html

Asimov, Isaac

http://www.io.org/ ~ toadaly/

Atwood, Margaret

http://uts.cc.utexas.edu/ ~ churchh/janeinfo.html

Austen, Jane

http://www.li.net/ ~ scharf/writers.html

Author Author (Top-notch index of Websites about and by various authors.)

http://julmara.ce.chalmers.se/SF_archive/Authorlists/

Author Bibliographies

http://imgnet.com:80/auth

Author Net

http://www.authorsspeak.com

Authors Speak

http://www.uio.no/ ~ mwatz/bey/index.html

Bey, Hakim

http://users.aol.com/pobronson/humor1.htm

Bronson, Po

http://www.tarzan.com

Burroughs, Edgar Rice

http://www.students.uiuc.edu/~jbirenba/carroll.html

    Carroll, Lewis

http://members.aol.com/pgmom/genespage.html

    Cartwright, Gene

http://world.std.com/~ptc/

    Carver, Raymond

http://icg.harvard.edu/~cather

    Cather, Willa

http://www.usis.usemb.se/sft/142/sf14213.htm

    Chandler, Raymond

http://www.vmi.edu/~english/chaucer.html

    Chaucer, Geoffrey

http://ws-mj3.dur.ac.uk/gkc/index.html

    Chesterton, Gilbert Keith

http://www.nltl.columbia.edu/users1/bkyaffe/wwwac/achome.html

    Christie, Agatha

http://ourworld.compuserve.com/homepages/NWeeger/clancye.htm

    Clancy, Tom

http://www.shu.edu/life/commence/95/hd3.html

    Clark, Mary Higgins

http://www.lib.virginia.edu/etext/stc/Coleridge/stc.html

    Coleridge, Samuel Taylor

http://www.interlog.com/~spiff/coupland

    Coupland, Douglas

http://www.en.utexas.edu/~mmaynard/Crane/crane.html

    Crane, Stephen

http://http.tamu.edu:8000/~cmc0112/crichton.html

    Crichton, Michael

http://www.catalog.com/mrm/poems

    cummings, e. e.

http://www.li.net/~scharf/defoe.html

    Defoe, Daniel

http://hum.ucs.edu/dickens/index.html

    Dickens, Charles

http://www.msu.edu/lecture

    Doctorow, E. L.

http://lal.cs.byu.edu:80/people/black/dickinson.html

    Dickinson, Emily

http://www.cis.ohio-state.edu/hypertext/faq/usenet/books/holmes/illustrated/faq.html

Doyle, Arthur Conan

http://www.cis.ohio-state.edu/hypertext/faq/usenet/books/holmes/list/faq.html

Doyle, Arthur Conan, The Holmes Booklist

http://web.syr.edu/ ~ fjzwick/dooley/

Dunne, Finley Peter

http://www.uta.fi/ ~ trkisa/duras/duras.html

Duras, Marguerite

http://www4.ncsu.edu/eos/users/m/mcmesser/www/eco.html

Eco, Umberto

http://www.yahoo.com/Arts/Humanities/Literature/Authors/Eliot_T_S_1888_1965_/

Eliot, T. S.

http://www.teleport.com/ ~ mzuzel/

Ellison, Harlan

http://www.mindspring.com/ ~ ledzep/

Farmer, Philip José

http://www.mcsr.olemiss.edu/ ~ egjbp/faulkner/faulkner.html

Faulkner, William

http://www.math.ru/ru/members/hohlov/hobby/books/f/

Francis, Dick

http://glyphs.com/millpop/95/annefrank.html

Frank, Anne

http://www.jeffnet.org/whitecloud/blovd.html

Gibran, Kahlil

http://www.charm.net/ ~ brooklyn/LitKicks.html

Ginsberg, Allan

http://www.suegrafton.com

Grafton, Sue

http://www.bdd.com/grisham

Grisham, John

http://pathfinder.com/twep/mysterious_press/hall/

Hall, Parnell

http://www.tiac.net/users/eldred/nh/hawthorne.html

Hawthorne, Nathaniel

http://sunsite.unc.edu/dykki/poetry/heaney/

Heaney, Seamus

http://fly.hiwaay.net/ ~ hester/heinlein.html

Heinlein Resource List

http://www.clark.net/pub/ahasuer/heinlein/heinlein.html

Heinlein, Robert A.

http://www.princeton.edu/~cgilmore/dune/

Herbert, Frank

http://www.ecnet.net/users/mujdh5/hughes.htm

Hughes, Langston

http://www.tiac.net/users/eldred/hjj/dm/daisy1.html

James, Henry

http://astro.ocis.temple.edu/~callahan/joyce.html

Joyce, James

http://www.charm.net/~brooklyn/LitKicks.html

Kerouac, Jack

http://wwwcsif.cs.ucdavis.edu/~pace/king.html

King, Stephen

http://www.accessnow.com/ll/welcome.html

L'Amour, Louis

http://tile.net/lessing/

Lessing, Doris

http://www.cache.net/~john/cslewis/index.html

Lewis, C. S.

http://sunsite.berkeley.edu/London/

London, Jack

http://arrogant.itc.icl.ie/AnneMcCaffrey.html

McCaffrey, Anne

http://cathouse.org:80/Literature/CarsonMcCullers/

McCullers, Carson

http://www.cs.umu.se/~dpcnn/eapoe/ea_poe.html

Poe, Edgar Allan

http://www.sas.upenn.edu/~smfriedm/exupery/

Saint-Exupéry, Antoine de

http://klinzhai.iuma.com/~drseuss/seuss/

Seuss, Dr.

http://the-tech.mit.edu/Shakespeare/works.html

Shakespeare, William

http://csclub.uwaterloo.ca/u/relipper/tolkien/rootpage.html

Tolkien, J. R. R.

http://www.lights.com/tolkien/timeline.html

Tolkien, J. R. R.

http://users.aol.com/Tolstoy28/tolstoy.htm

Tolstoy Library

http://web.syr.edu/ ~ fjzwick/twainwww.html

Twain, Mark

http://haven.ios.com/ ~ wordup/wilde/dorgray.html

Wilde, Oscar

http://web.msu.edu/lecture/wolfe.html

Wolfe, Tom

■

Index

C

Explorer, Microsoft Internet, 112
  HTML commands for, 114, 120–
    121, 134. *See also* HTML
e-zines, 91–95
  creating, 108–110
  defined, 92
  promotion tips, 97–99, 111–112
  See also magazines, online

F

fair use, 104
FAQs (frequently asked questions), 23,
  139
Feed, 10, 18–19
feedback, home page, 25–26
File Transfer Protocol (FTP), 143
  formatting tag links to, 126–127
First Virtual Holdings, 15–17
flaming, 44, 139, 140. *See also*
  netiquette
formatting tag, 115–136
  categories, 116
  coded character set, 130–136
  for images, 128–130
  for links, 125–128
  structure of, 116–118
  for text, 119–125
  See also HTML
Friendly Ghostwriter, The, 29–32
Fulton, Catherine, 11–12

G

Gambill, Herbert, 107–108, 110, 112
Gerrard, Jeff, 9
Gibson, William, vi, 139
GIF (Graphics Interchange Format), 128
  defined, 140
  See also image placement tag
glossary, 137–142
Gopher, 142
  defined, 139
  formatting tag links to, 126–128

Gordon, Hal, 29–32
Gray, Terry, 72
Gunther, March, 6

H

hardware
  ISDN line, 149–150
  modem, 140, 149–150
  requirements, 145–146, 149
  See also specific types
Harris, Muriel, 79
Hauman, Glen, 17
Heath, Dan, 95
Hewitt, John, 97–98
hexadecimal color codes, 134–136
home page
  benefits of, 21–28
  creating, 32, 112, 113–136
  defined, 152
  examples, 3–9, 29–37
  interactivity. *See* interactivity, home
    page
  See also publishing, online
host, Internet, 139
HotBot (search engine), 61
Hot Wired, 18–19
Howard, Beth, 8
HTML (hypertext markup language),
  113–136
  browser-specific, 113–114
  coded character set, 130–136
  defined, 113, 152
  sample page, 118
  See also formatting tag
HTTP (hypertext transport protocol),
  139, 142. *See also* hyperlink
hyperlink
  color codes, 134–136
  defined, 32
  in e-zine creation, 110
  formatting tags for, 125–128
  home page tips for, 26–27, 32

HTML commands, 118
in Shakespeare case study, 72

I

image placement tag, 128–130. *See also*
formatting tag
income, advertising, 17–19
Info*Seek* Guide (search engine), 61–62
infringement, copyright, 103–106. *See*
also copyright
interactive television, 150
interactivity, home page, 25
Amazon (bookstore), 87
National Geographic, 1–2
Salon, 96–97
SunSpot, 5
interlink. *See* hyperlink
Internet
address, 142, 150–151
defined, 137
hardware requirements, 145–146,
149
service providers, 143–149
Internet Explorer, Microsoft, 112
HTML commands for. *See also*
HTML, 114, 120–121, 134
Internet-In-A-Box (software), 152
Internet Newsroom, The, 150–151
Internet service provider (ISP), 143–150
and cable modems, 150
consumer checklist, 146–149
ISDN connection for, 139–140, 149–
150
Irish Times, 3
ISDN (Integrated Services Digital
Network), 139–140, 149–150. *See*
also Internet service provider
(ISP)

J

Jenks, Ken, 15–17
job hunting. *See* employment

journalism
resource list, 41
See also newspapers, online
JPEG (Joint Photographic Experts
Group)
defined, 128, 139
See also image placement tag
Junck, Mary, 5–6

K

Kessler, Lawrence, 3, 5
keyword
defined, 140
in research techniques, 58, 66, 68–70
Kinsley, Michael, 9–10

L

Labovitz, John, 92–94
Lawrence, Trevor, 49
Library of Congress (THOMAS) home
page, 66–68, 70
license agreement, 103–104. *See also*
copyright
link. *See* hyperlink
Listserv, 43–44
defined, 40
as research tool, 68
resource list, 41–42
search engine for, 41–42
Liszt (search engine), 41–42
Lycos (search engine), 59–60, 62

M

Macintosh publishing software, 110–111
Madsen, Hunter, 18–19
magazines, online, 9–10, 94–97
@NY, 32–37
publishing software, 110–111
publishing tips, 97–99, 111–112
resource list, 41
See also e-zines

interactive, 150
Internet box, 149
Telnet, 142
text formatting tag, 119–125
THOMAS (Library of Congress) home
    page, 66–68, 70
thread, newsgroup, 39
Time Warner, 13
Timmons, Thomas, 113–136
Toffler, Alvin, 68

U

Urban Desires, 10, 96
URL (Uniform Resource Locator), 152
    defined, 142, 150–151
Usenet newsgroup, 39–42
    categories, 40–41
    defined, 39–40, 142
    formatting tag links to, 126–128
    netiquette, 43–44, 139, 141
    as research tool, 68
    search engines for, 41–42, 59, 61–62
username, 142

V

virtual reality, 79

W

WAIS (Wide Area Information
    Searchers), 74
Watson, Tom, 32–37
Web browser. *See* browser, Web
WebCrawler (search engine), 64
Web site. *See* home page
Whatever Ramblings, 108
Windows 95, 146
Word, 19
World Wide Web (WWW)
    defined, 142
Writer's Dream (shareware), 111
Writers Net, 98–99

Writer's Nook News, 48
Writer's Resource Center, 97–98
Writer's Workshop, 48–49
writing lab, online, 79–83

Y

Yahoo
    advertising on, 18
    as research tool, 68–69

Z

zine. *See* e-zines; magazines, online
Zuzu's Petals Literary Resources, 4

Books from Allworth Press

Mastering the Business of Writing by Richard Curtis
(softcover, 6 × 9, 256 pages, $18.95)

The Writer's Legal Guide by Tad Crawford and Tony Lyons
(softcover, 6 × 9, 304 pages, $19.95)

Business and Legal Forms for Authors and Self-Publishers,
Revised Edition by Tad Crawford (softcover, 8½ × 11, 192
pages, $19.95)

The Writer's Guide to Corporate Communications
by Mary Moreno (softcover, 6 × 9, 192 pages, $18.95)

The Internet Research Guide by Timothy K. Maloy
(softcover, 6 × 9, 208 pages, $18.95)

The Internet Publicity Guide by V. A. Shiva
(softcover, 6 × 9, 208 pages, $18.95)

The Copyright Guide by Lee Wilson
(softcover, 6 × 9, 192 pages, $18.95)

Photography for Writers by Michael Havelin
(softcover, 6 × 9, 224 pages, $18.95)

Writing Scripts Hollywood Will Love
by Katherine Atwell Herbert (softcover, 6 × 9, 160 pages, $12.95)

Artists Communities by the Alliance of Artists' Communities
(softcover, 6¾ × 10, 224 pages, $16.95)

Please write to request our free catalog. If you wish to order a book, send
your check or money order to Allworth Press, 10 East 23rd Street, Suite
210, New York, NY 10010. Include $5 for shipping and handling for the
first book ordered and $1 for each additional book. Ten dollars plus $1
for each additional book if ordering from Canada. New York State residents must add sales tax.

If you wish to see our catalog on the World Wide Web, you can find us
at Millennium Production's Art and Technology Web site:
http://www.arts-online.com/allworth/home.html
or at **allworth.com**